DANCING
WITH AN
APOCALYPSE

TOM A. TITUS

Coastal Giant Press

©2021 Tom A. Titus
e-mail: tomtitus@tomtitus.com
website: www.tomtitus.com
blog: tomtitus.substack.com

All rights reserved. No part of this book may be reproduced, stored in a retrieval system, or transmitted in any form by any means without the prior written permission of the author except by a reviewer, who may quote brief passages to be included in a newspaper, magazine, or journal article.

Cover design by Ana Grigoriu-Voicu at
Books-Design.com

Cover photograph: Johnny Gunter house, Tom A. Titus

ISBN: 978-1-7333631-4-3

For Cara DiMarco (1957-2021)

*Yours was eclipse light,
intensity bent kindly
around black shadows.*

CONTENTS

Thank You! vi

In the Beginning (Wherein I Spin a
Story Explaining How All These
Musings Are Connected) 1

1. Cool Jelly 8
2. Habit 13
3. Firewood 17
4. Lady Slippers 19
5. Coping Strategies 20
6. Newts 22
7. Solitude 25
8. If A Tree Falls 28
9. Corvid 19 32
10. Father's Day 35
11. Glove Box 39
12. Deep Heat 41
13. Legacy 44
14. Brittle 48
15. Harbinger 51
16. Bobcat Skull 54
17. October Again 60

18. Mudroom	65
19. Post and Beam	71
20. Frost	76
21. Whole	79
22. Roof	82
23. Dinner	86
24. Bench	89
25. Evergreen	93
26. Conversations	97
27. Old Pickup	102
28. Precarious	107
29. Relationships	110
30. Bones	115
31. Pruning	118
32. Pulse	123
33. Unconformity	127
34. Dawn Chorus	134

Thank You!

Writing a book is a community effort even during the isolation imposed by a pandemic. For my community of online readers, I am profoundly grateful. Their names are numerous as night stars, their collective energy the inspiration for this book. Kimberlee Wollter is my editor, designer, soul mate, sounding board, and antidote for angst. My solo treks to the edge of the world are brief, and the trail always returns to her. Cathy Ward is the beta reader every writer loves, and her attentive reading and suggestions drew clarity out of chaos. Many pieces improved beneath the gentle hands of my Red Moons critique group: Grace Elting Castle, John Carter, Evelyn Hess, Cynthia Pappas, Kay Porter, and Kirsten Steen. Several essays appeared in *Nature Trails,* the monthly publication of the Eugene Natural History Society, where their rough edges were smoothed by the skillful editorial hand of John Carter. A warm embrace to Martha Gatchell for her spiritual and poetic influence on "Bobcat Skull." The essay "Cool

Jelly" was born during a collaborative residency with artist Emily Poole and hosted by the Spring Creek Project for Ideas, Nature, and the Written Word. Thank you to Eric Alan, Valerie Brooks, Sean Sharp, and Charlie Ward for those hug-less hours spent shouting through masks and across socially distant driveways and tables and decks. In the froth and foam of this turbulent world, my gratitude for all of you remains rock solid.

IN THE BEGINNING
(WHEREIN I SPIN A STORY EXPLAINING HOW THESE MUSINGS ARE CONNECTED)

The apocalypse overtook me in early March of 2020 while shopping for groceries at Costco. I was heading for the hills anyway, but not to escape the end of the world. Artist Emily Poole and I were about to embark on an artistic residency at the Cabin at Shotpouch Creek. Our time there was planned as a collaborative meander into the emerald convolutions of the Oregon Coast Range to draw and write the world of salamanders.

My wife had asked me to get toilet paper while I was out shopping. When I went to the usual place in the back of the store, that towering display of white rolls crammed into their suffocating plastic packages was gone. At first I thought they had moved it. After three exasperating laps around a building that seemed to have been built as a blimp hangar and was stuffed with everything you could possibly want, all oversized and overpackaged, I found a guy who looked official.

Do you know where the toilet paper is?

Nope. And if I did, I'd be sellin' it out of my pickup in the parking lot and makin' a lotta money.

I couldn't help myself. *No shit?*

All of this was a little unsettling. COVID-19 had barely arrived, caused by a viral 2 × 4 only 0.1 micron in diameter that was poised to whop humanity upside the head. Fear is a great salesperson, especially for toilet paper. Emily and I went to the cabin anyway—we knew there were plenty of paper products. We also knew there was no internet or phone service. We didn't know that this digital isolation would mean that the end of the world would arrive in blips and bytes of service gleaned from hikes onto the ridge above the valley. A trickle of COVID news became a torrent of shortages, cancellations, and school closures. We were amused, then dismissive, then incredulous, and finally downright depressed at the prospect of returning home to a "real" world that had very quickly become surreal. Emily and I thought about staying in the mountains with the salamanders. They didn't seem to care about any of it. The residency was supposed to have ignited an inferno of creativity. Instead, I didn't write for weeks.

Constant motion has always been my first line of defense against angst. My creative impulse was reduced to hard time with a chainsaw and hydraulic wood splitter. One day, wife Kim and daughter Laurel joined me at the Johnny Gunter place, a small family property with an orchard and a falling-down house deep in the Coast Range west of Eugene. We had come to split a pile of firewood from trees that were casualties of a big snowstorm the previous winter. In the evening, Kim and Laurel returned to town ahead of me. A cold breeze circled my solitude on the front porch. The old Douglas-firs on the north ridge began to speak the language of wind. Maybe theirs was the language of loss—their dead children had been split and thrown into an amber heap in the driveway.

One of my few remaining articles of faith is that our words lie within. But in the gathering COVID storm, I had blockaded their emergence into the larger world. The reasons for this are unclear to me. Maybe I felt that my stories needed a larger context within which to unfold, in the way that trilliums were now unfolding in the embrace of the early spring forest. Maybe I just needed a moment of stillness. Regardless, after Kim and Laurel left that evening the barrier began to fall away. I retrieved my phone from inside the old house and began thumb-typing a short piece entitled "Facing Down the Apocalypse." The title seemed to capture my feelings while sitting alone on a cold spring evening with darkness dropping like heavy black snow and everything "normal" in the outside world unraveling.

But no one faces down an apocalypse. The image implies that the end of the world is outside of us. In fact, the various firestorms that have transpired in these pandemic months are primarily caused by circumstances we carry inside ourselves. The horsemen are many: politics exemplified by assault rifles, shattered window glass, and a bumper sticker mentality that attempts to cook our differences down to catchy slogans; institutionalized racism and a refusal to face our deep-seated sense of other; overconsumptive societies spewing carbon that causes climate change that produces drought conditions where wildfires erupt thick as summer ticks on an emaciated deer; an unwillingness to deal with the biological reality of SARS-CoV-2, a virus driven by a simple loop of RNA that doesn't give a crap about our politics or creature comforts. One acquaintance facetiously asked *What apocalypse?* Hell, pick one. Regardless of which version of Armageddon we choose, we'll find an element of our own culpability and acquiescence.

All of us need to holster our self-righteous pointer fingers. Because the end of the world belongs to everyone. And since I am a part of everyone, part of this mess belongs to *me*. So I've chosen to dial up my inner demons and ask them to go dancing with the apocalypse. The pandemic has shortened my attention span to something resembling a gnat's breath, and the individual dances are short. The stage changes. Sometimes I'm hanging out in my neighborhood or occasionally traveling to a far-flung place such as the Grand Canyon. I'm usually self-conscious on the dance floor and often run for the heart of my beloved Coast Range where I swing and sway physically distant and alone at the Johnny Gunter place. The only steps I know are words strung into sentences that coalesce into paragraphs. These might be inspired by a meditative drip of winter rain from conifer boughs or the scream of a chainsaw engine. A silent congregation of mating newts or the whine of a portable lumber mill. The humbling verticality of Grand Canyon sandstone or the diminutive audacity of a calypso orchid. An outrageous neighborhood happy hour or another solitary dusk in the mountains.

These dances are improvised, unchoreographed, and idiosyncratic. Yet I shuffle along hoping for some universal chord of awareness. Dancing with an apocalypse is a process that calls for learning and cooperative movement. A gathering of voices in the way that chorus frogs buzz from the marshy valley floor, spurred to seek one another out by increasing angles of light and early spring rain. The frogs call with the certainty that life will continue beyond the edge of the world as humans now understand it. I'm calling, too; for a change in perspective, a widening of arms, inspiration to ensure that end times are only changing times. Each of these writings is a window into a dance hall of attentiveness during COVID times. Feel free to peek in. Voyeurs are welcome.

T.A.T.

1. COOL JELLY

While COVID-19 seizes the world by the throat, winter releases her gentle hold on the Oregon Coast Range. Emerald buds swell on bronze salmonberry canes. Alder leaf rot gives way to an early surge of sprouting larkspur and nettles. My artist colleague Emily Poole and I plunge downhill off a narrow trail, drawn toward the valley floor by standing water winking through chalky alder trunks.

Our steep descent to the pool is driven by an intuition for salamanders I have cultivated over a lifetime. We stand at the edge of the pond, seemingly at the edge of all things. The water is still as a meditation, a clear-eyed memory of the time when Shotpouch Creek rattled hard against the steep flank of the ridge on its hurried trip toward Mary's River. The creek has moved its gurgling energy to the east side of the valley, abandoning the pool to a trickle of spring water emanating from a sandstone crack somewhere up the ridge. Beavers long ago dammed the old channel with a matrix of peeled sticks now blackened by age. Elderly red alder trees encircle this stillness of water, their decayed trunks too large for our reaching arms, caped in moss sprouting licorice fern that resembles coarse green guard hairs. These ancient ones long ago lost their tops. Their vertical search for light has been taken up by limbs that push a ponderous load of lichens toward the March sun stretched thin above the southern ridge.

My intuition is correct. In the center of the pool, late morning light pierces the reflection of alders to reveal four northwestern salamander egg masses resting in a foot of cold water. Each cluster is a gelatinous fist clenched around an alder twig. Each mass contains about 80 quarter-inch embryos bent like dark commas around creamy yolk sacs. One mass is cratered on the surface. The embryos have been chewed out by a rough-skinned newt who now languishes innocently on the silty bottom.

The adult northwestern salamanders were here sometime last month. In that *before* time. That time when toilet paper and particle masks and paper towels and flour and all manner of other items remained on the store shelves. Emily and I would love to have seen those breeding salamanders, long and thick and brown as Havana cigars, a pair of parotoid glands bulging like misplaced thumbnails from either side of their heads. The male would have clasped a female from above, stroking her with his hind limbs and chin, an act of tactile and chemical foreplay. They might have swum together for days, occasionally surfacing for air, the male at times dismounting, nudging, remounting. He would have been persistent, patiently waiting for her clear but unspoken signal that she was ready to finalize their courtship. A few days later, implored by a bulge of fertile eggs, she would have glued her precious cargo around an alder twig, the jelly swelling with cold spring water.

From this shining morning at the edge of everything, forward-thinking daylight will stretch into spring, beyond what seems to be the imminent end of a human-centric world. The old alders will leaf out. Larkspur and nettle will press upward over the pungent rot of alder mulch. Raindrip will sing off burgeoning leaves, breaking the glassy pond with dimples. An intermittent silence of sunshine will be shattered by song sparrow and Pacific wren.

The salamander egg masses will host their version of furious spring growth. Each capsule will become progressively greener with a symbiotic alga. The relationship of embryos to alga is the ancient and ongoing reciprocity of symbiosis. Growing embryos will metabolize their allotment of yolk, producing waste products that are a nitrogen-containing superfood for the alga. The alga is photosynthetic, making carbon chains for energy and oxygen as a by-product. This oxygen will speed embryonic growth, because although the dense jelly of the egg mass protects the interior embryos from newt predation, it reduces their access to water-borne oxygen. In this small slice of stillness, life in the world of salamanders proceeds along its exuberant and orderly way, oblivious to the implosion of human affairs.

One brief but profound connection remains. I find a stick to extend my reach, step to the edge of the pond, and pull an egg mass gently toward my free hand. Silt that dusted the glass-like globe swirls free, sullying the crystalline water. Emily squats at the edge of the pool, cupping the cool jelly, smiling. Her words echo my thoughts: *I could hold this all day!*

We push the embryonic future of northwestern salamanders back into the pond, trusting their protection to a single-celled alga and an icy flush of spring water. For a moment, we are the reflection of ancient alders.

2. Habit

End of March at the beginning of the end of the world. Tomato sprites rise from a seedling tray into the sun-splashed afternoon. Two-inch stems support infant leaves no larger than sunflower petals. A brush of my hand releases the acrid aroma of summer. This is their habit of growth.

People say the verge of an apocalypse calls for hope. They say gardeners are an extraordinarily hopeful lot. I'm not so sure. Growing food seems more like a habit. Each winter I poke tomato seeds into sterilized soil with needled tweezers, repot seedlings in early spring, and liberate root-bound plants into a sea of May soil, dark and warm. Rhythm of grower and growth.

Our old cat is in the habit of living, even though he is dying. In gray rain he totters out to pee, wobbly skeleton knit together by mousy fur. He's a one-man cat who chose me in his youth. These days he sits on my lap, manages a purr. His breath smells like death, but his cells have a two-billion-year habit of living. They won't let him die.

I'm not in the habit of watching television. But the end of the world calls for distraction. An old George Carlin monologue. He says fuck a lot, speaks irreverently of the dead. He makes me laugh. Some time back his cells finally let him die.

Sun passes through a thin cloud sash on his arc toward the western ridge. I move tomato seedlings into four-inch pots and comfort their displaced roots by pressing my index finger onto musty soil as if searching piano keys for a forgotten tune.

Our cat needs help breaking the habit of living. At least that's what we think. Who really knows? I wrap and hold him in a tattered child's quilt. For 18 years he nursed the yellow yarn ties to fall asleep. My wife drives us to the vet. The end of the world requires that we wait in the car. Fingers of rain drum the roof. Gray bones struggle against my chest. We always wondered whether his quilt would outlast him.

Drugs take hold in the darkened room. He falls asleep in his blanket in my arms then meets the end of his world with an unobtrusive needle slipped into a hind leg.

Carlin's monologue rolls through my head. I'm not laughing. The apocalypse needs attentiveness, not distractions. The ancestors he derides are the collective habit of memory built from attentiveness. I decide Carlin can go fuck himself. But his cells broke the habit of living long ago.

Rain stops. Scooping the bundle from the back seat, failing body heat seeps through the old quilt into my arms. I carry remnants of cat and memory across the pasture of my childhood home. She carries the shovel and her own thoughts. We plant the bundle in wet earth where hillside meets pasture. I tell him I'll see him on the other side if there is one. There is plenty of soil to fill the hole. We cover the grave with a rain-soaked log and some rocks. Scavengers have a habit of finding dead things.

Driving home. Layers of sadness break apart in the western sky. A rainbow forms behind vaporous stacks of the pulp mill. Sun strains around a large cloud lying like a sideways hourglass across the foothills. A sideways hourglass cannot measure time. An upright hourglass cannot measure time either. Time cannot be measured. Dividing a cat's life into 18 years is as meaningless as parsing the differences between habit and ritual and hope.

A tattered quilt of darkness falls. The beginning of night at the end of the world. Sixty potted tomatoes of eleven varieties are arrayed in pots in trays. When they are watered they droop like dead things. I lift them gently from wet soil. They regain their upright habit.

I hope they grow.

3. FIREWOOD

It figures that a wet cold spring would be waiting at the edge of all we used to know. Morning overcast is locked against Sun like an iron door. I try to meditate, hope the drizzle will dampen those whirling sparks that pass for thinking. I enforce ten long breaths and give up. Some of us are wired for motion.

Mom rides out the apocalypse in the home where I grew up, which is perched on an ancient erosional terrace above the McKenzie River. Last fall one brother pulled several storm-toppled trees from the hillside into her pasture. This morning another brother and I meet to continue the process of converting logs into heat. I fall in love with his chainsaw, cheating on my own saw. The throaty roar of that Husky carving off rounds and spitting soft piles of sawdust at my feet is downright sexy. I promise my own saw that it's only for this morning.

My brother fires up his hydraulic wood splitter. A friend told me recently that hydraulics are a gift from the gods. I used to think he was joking. Even though the gods are dangling us by our feet over the precipice of the world, they have not left us powerless.

Obstinate downpour. All of the logs are bucked, so we both run the splitter. As humanity trips over the brink, I'm hoping for transformation, want to believe there is some helpful truth to two-cycle exhaust and sawdust creeping into my shirt and pain slithering into my forearms and the turpentine smell of cut fir and growing heaps of angular splits and busting my ass with my brother who is way better at ass-busting than I am. Yet in that search for a larger perspective, all I find is a downpour day washing brown rivulets off the pasture toward a river running toward a precipice of all that has been.

We break for lunch. Mom is very happy. Her boys are here.

4. Lady Slippers

They appear when I most need them, on this morning at the precipice of certainty at the threshold of vision along a two-track road squishing into shade. With thumb and forefinger I tip one face toward mine. Five petals flare like petite fingers pink above a mottled pouch, a tiny heart about to throb. Calypso orchid, aka *Calypso bulbosa*, aka thumb-size goblet of orchid sex nodding *yes*.

What's in a name at the edge of everything we know? As a child I knew them as lady slippers. In my aunt's hands, fistfuls of flowers formed aromatic bouquets wrapped gently in wet paper towels. She gifted them to family and friends, her version of love. Mom came to know them as threatened, taught us to hold them with only our eyes, and showed us that ownership is shared with hemlock, sword fern, and April moss.

Bees are duped by the promise of nectar the orchids don't produce. Some things aren't as sweet as they seem.

5. Coping Strategies

On days when I don't feel like writing, I go for a run. Running makes my knee swell.

When my knee swells from running, I've developed an ingenious strategy—I don't run. I don't write either.

When I don't feel like writing or running, I split firewood. Now my shoulder is sore from splitting wood. So I plant garden. Gardening makes my shoulder hurt, too.

When I don't feel like writing and can't run or split wood or plant garden, I dive into the slow-roasting depths of social media hell. The heat helps my knee and shoulder.

By afternoon, any pretense of productivity is washed away in the splash and churn of a sneaker wave of unchecked items and unfulfilled commitments. The Happy Hours have arrived. On the rocks.

I walk my rattle of bourbon and ice cubes across the street. Flames lick from a portable fire pit on the asphalt. My neighbors have been happy for several hours.

The kids are becoming feral. Their tribal ritual of roasting marshmallows for dinner has begun. So far there isn't a single third-degree burn.

I'm thinking about adopting a dog or a teenager. I need someone to blame besides my wife for the disappearing bourbon. She drinks gin.

Tomorrow will be another day stretching toward the end of the world we thought we knew.

Maybe I'll feel like writing.

6. Newts

There sure is a lot of sex at the end of the world, at least in some quarters. After a socially distant run on the chip trail, I seep sweat and stroll through the neighborhood park, pausing on a footbridge across a small creek. The air is a breathing thing. Ribs of willow and cottonwood exhale, unfurling the riverine smell of an April trout season from my youth. Afternoon sun angles from an emerald-eye sky, filling the clear pool where the stream pauses below the bridge.

In sun-split water at the edge of the bridge at the edge of the day at the edge of time, a gaggle of rough-skinned newts is absorbed with making more rough-skinned newts. Milk chocolate backs blend with basalt cobbles strewn on the bottom. Each cigar-size body is outlined with an apocalyptic trace of orange seeping from belly and tail. In the language of rough-skinned newts, orange tells a tale of toxicity. There is enough nerve poison in the skin of one adult newt to kill ten humans. No joke. But while they are poisonous, they aren't dangerous. Just don't eat one.

One newt has a dangle of pink nightcrawler the size of my pinky hanging half-swallowed from its mouth. This seems an ambitious undertaking. A squirming wad of five males vye for a single female in a tangle of submerged willow roots. Two others have already paired off, male clasping the female from above, a swimming undulation of sex that might continue for two days. Imagine it. Or don't. If the male fills the bill, the female will use her reproductive opening to grab a tiny plug of sperm that he will leave for her on the creek bottom. Afterward she'll glue fertile eggs to submerged twigs and return to the terrestrial neighborhood. Males will stay in the creek. They hope to mate again.

Hope. Now there's an interesting end-of-the-world word. I wonder whether newts know the difference between hope and instinct. I sure don't. Although I'm not enlightened in newt consciousness, it seems to me they simply show up in the creek looking for sex—two days of continuous sex if that's what it takes to extend the future of newts. There's some intelligence in that. Our human ancestors crawled out of the water a long time ago.

And even though we still carry a bit of newt brain with us, this up-and-coming end of our world requires that we emerge and blink newt-like into spring sunshine. We need a bigger-brained version of love, a love that reaches wider, a love worthy of all that gray matter we carry around in our skulls. We need a smarter kind of love that rises above all that squirming, jostling, shouldering, and pushing aside of others. These behaviors procreate a socioeconomic system that has evolved into something toxic and dangerous.

I hope we're smarter than newts.

7. Solitude

I ride the incoming swell of nightfall from the front porch of the Johnny Gunter house. The last logging truck rumbled out of the valley two hours ago. A single robin *chirrups* from the meadow that grows April green before me. An erratic west wind draws a steely overcast across the evening sky. Conifers sigh, go silent. The breeze is eddying beneath the hood of my dilapidated down parka, whirlpooling around my squinched eye sockets. Chili and a piece of last fall's winter squash cool quickly in a bowl next to my chair as the thermometer on the tattered shake wall drops to 46 degrees. The temperature might as well be 20. I shiver here at the brink of all things: house, meadow, darkness, all of my known world..

In the suburbs I am rarely alone, even in this new culture of separation. This is good. Our human need for companionship has been wrapped into the coil of our chromosomes by 55 million years of primate evolution. Yet even with this longstanding history of sociality, our ancestors understood the need for solitude. Occasional vision quests are necessary.

This evening there is seclusion in these crenulated mountains, ancient beings incised by water into canyons that shelter a multitude of other beings within their steep-sided depths. Here there is space for shutting down the judgment centers of the brain required by civilized existence. The neurological partitions that keep my well-ordered world well ordered become porous. I can peek cautiously into unplumbed depths without getting vertigo.

And yet a cold dusk wind in the Coast Range can be the loneliest damned thing in this raw and uncertain world. There was a time when I knew the difference between solitude and loneliness. Gradually the boundary between the two became translucent. They now bleed as one into my solitary soul like this chilling nightfall. I should go inside, turn on the lights, fire up the woodstove, and read words written by someone else. Instead, I sit in this chair with my cold dinner, spread my arms around the gray wind, gather in the ache. My inner demons begin to swirl, find their voice. This seclusion is the fuel I need for imagination, much like a rock climber needs adrenaline or fatigue drives an endurance athlete.

High tide of nightfall. Wind quiets itself. My bow line unravels, and I separate from the shore of civilization. From somewhere in the east, suburban lights reach out to rescue me, then lose their way in dark canyons. I am adrift in a silent blackness certain as death.

8. If a Tree Falls

Last evening a tree tipped over the edge of the world as I know it. The Douglas-fir died in exactly the spot I directed, sent there with a chainsaw and hand-winch. I am not an expert faller of trees, although for several years in my youth I made my living dropping lodgepole pine around what in those days were million-dollar homes. No serious harm was done back then. However, there was a small issue of a tree landing on a high-voltage line that knocked out the power in three towns. This momentary but monumental lapse in judgment might explain my lifelong practical and theoretical difficulty with electricity.

The tree I fell yesterday was 30 inches on the stump, 60 feet high, and only 26 years old. Its exuberant life began the same year my family and I restarted our own lives by moving back to Oregon. This rampant growth was possible because a small seed helicoptered in and took root just downhill from the blueberry patch at the Johnny Gunter place. The tree undoubtedly benefited from surplus summer water and fertilizer. Because I have been caring for the blueberries for the past ten years, I take some of the credit for those growth rings, some of them over half an inch wide.

The tree's early demise was also my responsibility. Over the decades I have killed tens of thousands of trees, most of them while working as a precommercial thinner. Now age has brought me to an uncomfortable juncture. These days I dislike the killing, but I'm still compelled to yank the starter cord on a chainsaw and let it bite through the lizard skin bark of a living thing, leaving resinous blond bits of tree flesh scattered in needle duff. In this case, the Douglas-fir's boisterous reach was beginning to shade the blueberries and summer vegetable garden. In yet another of those thousand daily compromises we make to remain alive on this death-filled planet, I took the gangly adolescent down.

Other reasons drove me to take the life of this ascendant being. Two winters ago I had a conversation with the old house, which is in a horrible state of disrepair. The house agreed to a repair job, as long as the lumber came from the nearby forest. This promise required that I become co-owner of a portable sawmill, in addition to having chainsaws and falling wedges and other implements of tree death. Although the mill has provided the wherewithal to transform trees into beautiful lumber, my conversations with the trees have now become more difficult—a few of them must die to fix the house. Before I fired up the saw, I explained all of this to the Douglas-fir and apologized for what I was about to do. Conversations with houses and trees can take a long time. While words come rapidly to me, my listening skills with nonhuman beings need some refinement.

In this year at the end of everything I thought I knew, scuttling along on the trailing edge of my life, I'm having even harder conversations with myself. Why do I persist in pouring energy into this outpost in the Coast Range, this human-made bubble of sunlight and space, only to slow its inevitable return to needle and leaf? The answer is complex and weaves together six generations of ancestors and descendants with conscious connections to this place. There are wounds to people and the forest that need healing. Meanwhile, my ego slinks around the edges like a stray cat, manifesting as a desire to keep the house intact for another generation. The forest and house and I are drawn together by healing and death. We travel a road that extends beyond the edges of our small lives.

9. CORVID 19

My mask is stuffed in the glove box of the pickup. I can't get any more socially and physically distant than this house in the heart of the Coast Range, somewhere inside the slosh and roil of its left ventricle. A strange north wind limbers big trees on the ridge. They sigh with the effort, a sound of ancient wood resisting this new direction, this odd bend to their boughs.

From the valley floor, Raven gives voice to the strangeness of the evening. The evening must be very strange because Raven repeats himself. Seven short croaks. Pause. Seven more. Reprise. Raven has no human name. He isn't Number 19, either. He is in the human-designated bird family Corvidae, our name for jays and crows. Corvids have big brains, count, use tools, recognize human faces, and talk a lot. Ravens even use humans as tools and sometimes lead hunters to their quarry, hoping to feast on the offal-filled aftermath.

"Corvid" looks and sounds a lot like "COVID." But COVIDs aren't as smart as corvids. Viruses also use humans, but their exploitation is a unidirectional machine approach. A handful of genes on a single strand of RNA implicates itself into our cells. Maybe after a few billion years of evolution, SARS-CoV-2 will learn the creative manipulation of ravens, who entwine themselves into the ways of other species with outcomes beneficial to both parties.

Occasionally I reciprocate to the ravens on behalf of humans by feeding them various animal remains. A few days back I found a mole dead as a gray stone in the meadow grass, expired for reasons I can never know. I placed the furry fist of her body face down on an altar of rocks at the edge of the meadow, her pink outsized hands outstretched. In this canyon-creased world where all things are part of an ongoing ecological conversation, everyone is both eater and eaten.

Raven's nameless outpourings continue from below. He is smart and has something to say. I decide to strike up a conversation. *We haven't talked for a while. Why don't you come on up?*

He moves to the firs below the garden, clucks a few times. I remain silent. The Old

Ones on the ridge sigh again, a cool exhalation of needles that brushes against my right cheek. His Blackness rises into the breeze, charcoal oars rowing across the camas-colored sky. Thirty feet above me he brakes and hovers in an airborne hunch. A croak emerges from my throat that sounds like *hello*. Wings extend as if reaching toward the edge of night. He reverses course, *whooshing* back toward the valley bottom on that mysterious north wind.

10. FATHER'S DAY

On Father's Day, my plane to Seattle roars from the runway, nose pointing into morning clouds shoaled against the Coburg Hills. My father loved all things airborne. He was a pilot who owned two small planes in his lifetime. Me? Not so much. But right now, speed is paramount. This plane is already two days late leaving for New Jersey, and I need to be there ASAP to help my son and family move home to Eugene. For now, I'm over any pretense that seamless on-demand air travel is anything but a relic of our privileged past. I'll be happy to let it go.

The prop churns skyward four feet from my window, engine painted in garish orange and blue, adorned with the grimacing face of the Boise State fighting bronco. I must be on the team plane, freed up in the off-season to fly unathletic people traveling in pandemic times. In a field of meadowfoam below, bee boxes cluster like squared-off swans. A woman across the aisle coughs incessantly into her mask. I turn back to my window and discretely check the seal around my own N100 mask. Suddenly I'm grateful for that feeling of suffocation.

The plane climbs steadily into cloud puff. Jeffrey Foucault's tune "Californ-i-a" rolls through my head. *"Well I guess ... you're gone ... to Californ-eye-ay, and I don't ... expect ... you'll be coming back this way ... real soon."* His guitar work is stellar. No one can hear me above the roar of the props or see my mouth moving behind the mask, so I hum the low notes from his E2 string. The throb of music and engine vibration resonates in the anxious cavern of my chest, massaging my heart. We break above the cloud layer. Loowit (Mt. St. Helens) is a cratered gray barnacle jutting above a cloudscape of hummocks and fissures. I drift into a contemplation of good guitar work, COVID, volcanoes, and gray spaces.

At Sea-Tac Airport there is 99% conformance to masks. A woman waits in the shuttle line with her two kids, all three of them clad in hats, gloves, masks, and hazmat suits. I didn't know they made hazmat suits for kids. Then a barefaced loudmouthed 30-something piles into our shoulder-to-shoulder shuttle train. Maybe he forgot his mask. Or maybe he's just a self-centered asshole. His reasons don't really matter to the family in hazmat suits and his other captives.

The departures board sends me to the wrong gate, but I find my jet to Newark anyway. We become airborne to the west, then make a climbing turn eastward. At 15,000 feet, Koma Kulshan (Mt. Baker) glowers against a glacier sky, crystalline, imposing. Somewhere over North Dakota, cruising level and level-headed at 35,000 feet, this ridiculous high-speed tube of pressurized aluminum steers north away from a solemn row of vaporous anvils, thunderclouds towering to 40,000 feet. Massive thunderstorms are one of five things I miss from my ten years in the Midwest, the other four being fireflies, blue jays, cardinals, and copperheads.

Three hours later the plane levels, sinks, then circles the languid Atlantic. Afternoon thunderstorms are mercifully distant, sparing me the certainty of motion sickness. My stomach sinks anyway, anticipating another crowd of COVID-carrying humans in the Newark airport. But the place is mostly barren. You could shoot a cannonball down the concourse without hitting anyone. The vending machine miraculously spits a train ticket into my waiting hand on the first try, and I'm aboard the next shudder and sway to Princeton.

Happy Father's Day to me, oh father of my son who is the father of my grandsons.

11. Glove Box

Contents of a glove box at the edge of everything:

1 shed rattlesnake skin
 (disintegrating)

1 road-flattened ring-necked snake
 (in several pieces)

1 crushed robin egg
 (turquoise fragments too numerous to count)

1 mummified bat
 (still intact!)

3 lighters
 (I don't smoke)

3 pairs of reading glasses
 (my eyesight isn't that poor)

1 Oregon highway map
 (don't need no soothing GPS voice)

1 manual for car stereo
 (long since dead)

1 ice scraper
   (now replaced with an old credit card)

Numerous insurance cards
   (all expired)

Components of small first aid kit
   (no longer a kit)

Smattering of useful items
   (toilet paper, flashlight, pickup manual)

No gloves are evident.

12. DEEP HEAT

Dusk in deep summer. Both mowers are busted. Forward gear on the lawn tractor sounds like chattering teeth, and the drive chain on the brush mower is disconnected and stretched like a dark snake in the dirt of the garage floor. With power tools silenced, the weeds are making their move. A collective pungency of dandelion, Queen Anne's lace, and meadow knapweed swirl together and nip at the heels of escaping light. Raven caws and circles the deepening pool of sky. The temperature has fallen 20 degrees in two hours. A cool breath of early autumn dances across my salty neck. There is an easy-going irony in this attentiveness, a seasonal moment that carries me gently into the future.

In the quiet reek of weed whiff and day fade, I settle in with my journal and a cold burn of bourbon on jingling ice. In this COVID-fissured summer, I have been resistant to keyboards, unwilling to transform words into bytes and phosphors. Other projects fly thick and fast as August gnats: rebuild the back deck, remove honey from beehives, transform cabbage into sauerkraut, save lettuce and kale seeds. There have been berries berries berries: two gallons of Ollalie blackberries today, twenty pounds of U-pick blueberries yesterday, two wild blackberry pies, and a batch of jam earlier in July.

This evening I sorted and stacked the first lumber milled from trees ravaged in the snowstorm of 2019. After a lengthy discussion with the old house who decays quietly behind me, I promised to rebuild it with lumber milled from the surrounding forest. This is a great idea, except that I don't know how to run a sawmill or build a house. Always those damned details ... but I'm learning.

These are my arcane obsessions and diversions from a world where everything and nothing seem to hold hands and leap together from one day to the next. Somewhere deep in my chest is a space the size of a rough-cut 2 × 6 that bristles with unspeakable anger, a shield for my unspeakable fear. My newly interracial family must persist in a society where discourse has become as dysfunctional as a compound fracture. The collective conversation has devolved into rifles, tear gas, leaf blowers, incendiary devices, and federally sanctioned abductions. Bracketing all of this social discord are my grandsons, one with albinism and the other African/Puerto Rican, bookends of pigment. I want to tuck them away into this quiet fold in the mountains, wait it out. Here, the days and nights flow closer to the ground and seem to make a little sense. There is danger, too, but it's mostly of one's own making.

Yet all I can reasonably do amidst the chaos is keep breathing, long and purposeful. The way Douglas-fir reach upward with silhouette arms in supplication to another day now fading on human foibles. Or how Moon rises above the eastern tree line, luminous as a song, her pale shoulder carrying Jupiter above this torn and weary world. Even a termite, its ant-like body the color of a worn penny, flutters flat wings on my journal page with grace. This gaping maw of summer fills the bucket of my heart. Fear begins to flush and spill over the rim and onto the waiting meadow.

13. Legacy

The August sunrise is no bullshit. No nuanced orange, no soft pink feathers spreading seductively westward. Just a hot silver dollar glare, Lady Liberty promising to deliver on triple-digit heat. Today is our grandparenting day. On a hot weekend in COVID times, people will be inundating local rivers and lakes, more anxious to cool off than to keep their distance. We decide to make an end run around the crowds and load the two grandsons, a soccer ball, swimming trunks, and a few indoor games into an air-conditioned car for a backroad trip to the Johnny Gunter place.

Our upstream world is near the headwaters of Upper Smith River, and access to kid-friendly water is limited. But other options abound. The boys relish the last of the ripe blueberries. In honor of *Mr. Putter and Tabby Pick the Pears,* we zing windfall apples over the fence for the deer and bears. Chris taste-tests every one. On the front porch, the blue dial of the Douglas County Electric thermometer pushes on beyond 100. The house is still cool, so Edmund and his grandmother hide inside and play a made-up dice game.

Chris and I drag out a bucket and hose and wash the car. He sprays with wild and random abandon while I sponge down hot metal. Washing a vehicle with a two-year-old is not the purview of efficiency experts, but the car ends up very clean. Then everyone is outside, boys squealing and chasing grandparents and each other with 100 feet of garden hose and a spray nozzle. The cool spring water is a gravity-fed gift from the mountains to two young boys, their grateful grandparents, and the summer-parched grass.

We drive toward town and a pizza place by the river. The freeway between Cottage Grove and Goshen is straight as split cedar. Edmund plays arithmetic games in his head. Chris sleeps. I have a few minutes to slip off into the ridges and valleys of my brain. I've grown to love the Johnny Gunter place more than any other, even more than the rural 25 acres where I grew up in the McKenzie River valley. It's the last Gunter family property on Smith River, where my great-grandfather settled in 1888. I'm already shepherding this legacy into the future. I mow the meadow, grow a garden, prune the orchard, keep water flowing from the spring. I'm moving ahead with plans to rehabilitate the crumbling house with lumber milled from the surrounding forest. This facelift might be enough to keep it standing for another generation.

Then what? My living window on this vibrating blue-green world is beginning to close. My children don't share the depth of my attachment to this place, and I will not foist my need for legacy onto them. The Buddhist teaching of impermanence is the only rational way to proceed on this earth that for a short time holds the container of our life. But the bowl sloshes over with needs and desires. I still hope—that someday after I've moved on, two boys who squealed and sprayed mountain spring water across scorched August grass will emerge from the forested tunnel of the driveway into the shimmering meadow, see the house standing on the left, notice green summer apples drooping in the orchard on the right, hear the chitter of barn swallows swooping into the garage. I hope they can know that some small part of their material world remains whole and good.

Edmund asks if we can come back next week.

14. Brittle

Early evening at the drought-tattered end of a Coast Range summer. A few crickets raise their shrill buzz from uncut knapweed above the parking area. Long-angled sunlight passes over parched meadow grass, highlighting new clearcuts on the ridges across the valley. Four band-tailed pigeons flap frantically toward the drooping sun, trapped beneath an arch of blue glass. I could reach up and break an end off Moon's fragile crescent slung over the western ridge. She would return whole and healed tomorrow evening.

A doe arrives with two fawns half her size, their birth spots fading. From across the meadow, they pin me with dark-eyed stares and a glisten of wet noses in dry air. The evening softens. Then one of the fawns reaches under the doe to nurse, and she kicks it hard in the head. *No milk and warm fuzziness for you, buddy. Better get busy and browse.* They wander in a wide circle to my right, headed for the windfall Gravenstein apples outside the orchard fence. The doe's life has not been all bliss. She turns and I see that her summer-blond hair is marked with a dark scar above and behind her right shoulder. She is teaching her offspring to survive.

My time in this quiet refuge is more often reflective than transcendent. This evening I feel brittle on the inside, fragile as the heat-ravaged grass. Haphazard cracks are forming under the pressure of COVID and politics and a society sickened as much by systemic racism as the pandemic. Add to all that a moment on a recent outing when a long-time friend unknowingly waylaid me with an offhand remark meant to underscore the supposed lesser intelligence of people in my hometown of Springfield. *What did you just say?* She didn't hear my question, and the moment passed after only an eye roll from my wife.

Sometimes I want to grab people by the lapels. Get up in their faces. Quietly explain to them in a no-bullshit monotone how deep and wide resentment can grow in the cesspool of their shit-don't-stink classism. I want to tell them their classism is fundamentally similar to the racism that now threatens to shatter this house of glass that Lyndon Johnson once dubbed "The Great Society." I want to tell them that their intrinsic attitudes are a lousy metric for the worth of others. Maybe it's a good thing lapels are out of fashion.

Twilight. The slivered and silvered moon intensifies. More crickets join the buzzing frenzy to find a mate before fall frost ends their short lives. My breathing softens as darkness seeps in from the forest, beads up, gathers in pools, then spreads across the sunburned meadow like cooling sweat. And yet beneath this supple sea of darkness, hard edges lurk like a ship-eating atoll.

15. Harbinger

Seven a.m. at this falling down house in the mountains. The front porch thermometer reads 46 degrees. Yesterday's weather report in town said were headed for 95, almost a 50-degree swing in less than eight hours. Three-quarter Moon wanes and trips west across a blue-tone sky. Sun peeks above the eastern ridge, basting dark conifers in orange sauce. This year's cone crop perches in the other-worldly needle glow like thick flocks of brown finches. The oscillating sprinkler in the garden pours forth a rhythmic *pishing*. *Quick-quick-slow-slow, quick-quick-slow-slow, send-ing wa-terrr, send-ing wa-terrr*, splishing spring water from the ridge onto winter squash vines, collards, and tomatoes. Painted Mountain corn stands watch, already shucked and drying on the stalks. A northern flicker cheers in the new day. Steller's jays squawk their approval of the morning as they glide from fir to fir, ascending the ridge one tree at a time. An invisible doe snorts from the clearcut next door, presumably at me, but who knows? Maybe she's been interrupted by the resident bear who is out demolishing logs for grubs.

The quietude of September has always given me the willies. September is a transitional month, a liminal pry bar slipped between summer and autumn. A long time ago I tripped over September and fell into clinical depression. For me, there are two good things about having been depressed. The first is that it ended. The second is that I've learned to read those nudges of imminence and take steps to mitigate a full-blown meltdown. In this hugless summer of hidden smiles, hidden people, and absurd political theater, somehow I have managed to maintain a reasonable state of emotional well-being.

But last week my early warning system sent out the alert. The cogs were slipping a bit. In this covidian apocalypse, Elizabeth Gilbert's words on the mythology of the so-called "suffering artist" seem especially suitable. She maintains that we cannot effectively share our gifts when in a debilitated state. We also become gawd-awful company. The world is already a gawd-awful suffer-fest and doesn't need my contribution of angst. This deteriorating outpost in the Coast Range has all the necessary elements for my peculiar version of emotional mitigation: an enforced vacation from the news, lots of time outside, and ass-busting physical labor.

Sweating will come later. Right now I burrow into my coat and hear a sound like a breeze on boughs sifting down from the old growth on the ridge. But the trees aren't moving, and it's too early in the day for wind. Maybe the Old Ones have gathered in a collective murmur, some arboreal comment on the dying summer. They are communicating, whether or not we hear their words. This "tree speak" is now established science, thanks in part to the pioneering research of forest ecologist Suzanne Simard.

Suddenly the sprinkler goes silent. A faint whisper of moving air strokes my face. The trees on the ridge had been speaking. Theirs is the language of wind sliding off an invisible ridge of high pressure to the north, a harbinger of heat on a morning when my fingers are stiff with cold.

16. Bobcat Skull

Last day of this catastrophic summer. I had just returned to the Johnny Gunter place from my annual elderberry excursion. The evening was thick with the smell of sunshine on damp forest. Duck flank clouds feathered in from the west. A breeze easy and soft as the sky stirred the ridges in ways I could feel but not see. Sun tripped and fell over the western ridge, and the fading light intensified the pulse of cricket buzz. A sip of icy beer bubbled and snapped in my mouth.

On a good day of elderberrying I can fill two five-gallon buckets in an afternoon. That's enough to make about fourteen quarts of juice, which is purple and thick and loaded with antioxidants that are good for the immune system. Antioxidants seemed especially important now that the coming winter was beginning to look like it would become a muddy viral minefield. The berries hang in clusters from clumps of woody stems that I call trees but seem more like bushes. They thrive in the sun-drenched aftermath of clearcuts and fires then fade away as growing conifers rob them of direct sunlight. About eight years ago, my elderberry place became choked with second growth and brush. When I mentioned this in a fireside chat with my neighbors Jerry and Martha, Jerry gifted me a new patch. Since then my elderberry seasons had been filled with easy abundance. When Jerry died and left Martha and the rest of us behind, visiting his elderberry place became a way for me to connect with him.

This year things changed. The pickup and I twisted along the two-track logging road through an old forest along the creek bottom. But when the road emerged into the clearcut where the elderberries thrived, Scotch broom pressed so tightly against the cab that the rearview mirrors folded inward. I parked in my usual place at the end of the road, grabbed one of the buckets, and ventured into the brush. My bare arms were immediately bloodied by Armenian blackberries that strangled the steep bank below the road. One Scotch broom higher than my head snatched my hat. Picking even a few clusters of elderberries was a struggle. I began to realize that filling two buckets would be an all-day project.

I remained hell-bent and obstinate despite all the signs telling me that the time for picking this patch of elderberries had passed. I finally paused in a small opening where tawny September grass bent dry and frail around my knees. Potawatomi elder Robin Kimmerer teaches us to ask permission. Asking opens us to gratitude, to taking only our share. In the case of elderberries, my permission has always come with guidelines: pick only the berries you can reach without damaging the tree, and take only the ripe ones. These small rules ensure there will be plenty left for the band-tailed pigeons and bears who need the fruit to fatten for migration or hibernation. But I had forgotten to ask. I was thrashing around in the blood-letting brush, and was focused on both the scarcity of elderberries and the time that remained of the vanishing afternoon.

One good thing about forgetting to ask is that you can remember, then forgive yourself and move forward. I raised my arms in surrender and looked toward the ground. A log, bare-skinned and gray, stretched in the grass before me. On the end of the log sat a bobcat skull, wide-eyed, bulbous, the color of fog, canine teeth arching prominently from the upper jaw. There was no obvious explanation for how the skull had arrived on this incongruous perch. Maybe it was a gift from Raven. Or perhaps I had placed it there myself on a September outing years ago (having a short memory sometimes makes it easier to be a mystic). For some reason, or for no reason at all, I was compelled to cradle the softball-size roundness in my hands and kiss it on the forehead. I confessed to the skull that I could use a little help here and asked if it would mind riding in my bucket for a short while. My elderberry lot in life improved immediately. Of course it did. I stopped struggling through the brush and stayed on what was left of the overgrown road. One fruit-laden tree seemed to bend toward my bucket. When the skull became submerged in berries, I brought it to the surface and buried it again with more clusters.

As the bucket filled, my solitary picking became a meditation. I began to realize this would be a one-bucket elderberry year. There was also a growing awareness that this would be my last year to pick in this place Jerry had given me. In my mind I told him that a single-bucket end to our elderberry connection bothered me. He told me to get over it, even though in life he was too gentle a soul to utter words as harsh as those.

The bucket was full when I spotted a few smoky-gray elderberry clusters the size of dinner plates. They hung low to the ground and just off the road. I didn't think Jerry would mind if I heaped the bucket. I wasn't driven so much by greed but by a desire to extend this time with my friend. When I started off the road, a small log hidden by blackberry vines tripped me up. The bucket handle twisted off, spilling the top six inches of berries into some dead grass. The bobcat skull rolled back toward the road. I swore hard, managed to gather up most of the spilled berries, and returned the skull to what seemed to be its rightful place atop the harvest. Fighting all signs that the picking needed to end, I left the bucket at the road and collected those last low-hanging clusters into my hands. I returned to the bucket, took the ivory roundness of the skull in one hand, and with the other smeared it with my last bullheaded handful of berries. Curves of bone glistened faintly lilac in the lengthening angle of evening light.

At the Johnny Gunter place, the wispy evening continued to settle. A sickled moon sliced through a cloud-feather sky now reflecting the lavender hue of elderberries. When I rose, an I-am-no-longer-young ache creaked from my bones. The smell of a sweaty afternoon blossomed from my T-shirt. For some reason my beer can was empty. I gathered my things. Locked the house. Then I took the bobcat skull down the road to Martha.

17. OCTOBER AGAIN

Despite all my years of experience and forewarning, October's frothy fulmination of overcast mornings, first rainstorms, contracting day length, glistening chanterelles, and spawning salmon is messing with me. Again. In October I often feel as though I'm teetering along a ridgetop narrow as a knife's edge with a clear view into the valleys on either side. One valley is sunlit and verdant with opportunity and potential. The other is quieted by shadows and death. Mix in a smidgeon of wildfire smoke, political chaos, and a virus that is agnostic to the needs of humanity, and what could be easier to navigate? Despite the chaos, October is also the time when death and possibility stimulate the churning alchemy of neurotransmitters in my brain to stir up new ways of thinking and being in the world. I love October.

The deer don't care about my roiling brain chemistry and stop in for a visit. Beyond the front window of the Johnny Gunter house, that doe with the scar on her right shoulder materializes from the tree line just below the grapevines. After retrieving my warmed-up dinner, I hesitate before heading out to my customary evening perch on the porch. I'm the irregularity here, the occasional interloper not integrated into the daily ebb and flow. I don't want to disrupt her routine. But the gathering evening gets the better of me, and I slip outside and into my plastic lawn chair on the porch. The doe moves around the garden fence, catches me in the dark glisten of her stare, antenna ears up. Quickly I look down into my bowl and keep eating. She seems satisfied that I'm not in the business of eating her and goes back to browsing. A yearling follows. Together they wander toward the edge of the meadow in search of windfalls beneath the unkempt apple trees outside the orchard fence. Her spotted twins are not in evidence. In deference to my struggling neurons, I decide against any contemplation on the absence of the twins.

Darkness is fully formed by eight o'clock. The moonless sky is riddled with stars. Milky Way tips brilliantly sideways. I decide that the gape and yawn of blackness between prickled lights should be left to ponder on another evening, in another season. Back in the house, my eyes shutter down. I go to bed, skip my evening read, and fall asleep in five breaths.

I'm wide awake at 3 a.m. That's what happens when you go to bed at 8 p.m. Beyond the living room window, a thin meringue of clouds slides southwest beneath the gentle light of a three-quarter moon. I pick up my journal and sit on the old couch, which is covered by a bedsheet. A battery-powered clock ticks loudly over my right shoulder. Power outages are frequent here, and a battery-powered clock is the only way to keep time, as if time could ever be kept. Seconds tick into single file, following the cloud drift to some nameless place where time and clouds go to die.

Even when the power is on, we have difficulty harnessing it in the various rooms. About half of the sockets and switches have ceased to channel electrons to perform their various duties. This morning I'm reading next to a lamp plugged into the wall because the last functioning light socket in the living room ceiling is dead. Another rodent has apparently taken refuge in the attic and chewed through one more of the wires that were still intact. If your teeth grew ceaselessly, you'd chew on wires, too.

Dark morning stillness is shattered by engine roar and tire whine from the first logging truck of the day flying down the road below the house. My left hand is inexplicably clenched against my stomach. Fingers unfurl and flex. A deep breath gathers new oxygen that might illuminate other tautness hiding in my body, in the way Moon illuminates clouds or stillness illuminates passing seconds. I want to send my tension to that place where passing clouds and seconds go. The road back to sleep is a long one.

Daylight. The front porch thermometer registers a balmy 56 degrees. There must have been a shortage of space in the place where those scudding wee hour clouds were headed. Now they are backed up like jammed traffic into a solid overcast. A cup of coffee and a bowl of hot oatmeal with honey and apples warm my fingers. Forty small birds swoop in like a swarm of bees, silhouetted by gauzy gray. They alight in a cluster of three tall firs between the meadow and the clearcut next door. Douglas Squirrel chatters, facing down some threat known only to her.

Paradoxically, the overcast has lifted me from my downcast. Coffee and oatmeal help, too. I'll likely just react to the day. Maybe erect some 4 × 4 posts for the mill shelter I'm building by the garage. Load some rusty metal fencing and pipes into the trailer and haul them back to town for a last satisfying *clang* into the recycling bin. Pick some apples ahead of our family cider pressing day this coming week. No one is here to transmit their viral droplets. No one cares if I am politically aware. No one will consciously or subconsciously notice the color of my skin or see me stop and stare into space. No one is watching, not even my phone, that watcher of all things. It mercifully lost contact when I dropped off the ridge on the way here. For this day I am captive only to my thoughts. And in October my thoughts are not well trained. They run on a very long leash.

18. Mudroom

The day after an October downpour, overcast draped heavy on the mountains, occasionally fused into an afterthought of mist. Tomorrow will be our traditional Cider Day, when all the surplus apples at the Johnny Gunter orchard are converted into gallons of amber drinkability. People will be coming, all of them family, all of them grateful to occupy the last Gunter outpost on Upper Smith River. But this year I was cringing. The property is a junk heap. Like osprey who add yearly layers of sticks to a nest, the place has become jammed with clutter accumulated across the decades by people (myself included) who throw *nothing* away.

No place in the house has amassed more stuff than the six-foot-wide space between the porch and the living room. We call it the mudroom, a genteel moniker given the current state of affairs. Step inside from the front porch, and you are smacked upside the nostrils by the musky aroma of woodrat piss. Window sills are littered with black BB-sized turds of a Douglas squirrel who lives in the attic and makes frequent trips down the stairs to survey his domain through windows grayed by thirty years of heirloom dust and cobwebs. Walls bristle with rusty nails slung with pieces of dog chain, pulleys, galvanized washtubs, rain clothes brittle with age, decaying lawn chairs, and pruning tools of various sorts. That's the organized part. The floor is an unfathomable jumble of old shoes, rubber boots, bird netting, plastic buckets with and without contents, rolls of leftover linoleum, poisons for weeds and rodents and slugs, bags of fertilizer, a sack of concrete now rock hard, an extra chainsaw with fuel and bar oil, and a weed eater. Axes, shovels, digging bars, rakes, a pitchfork, and a post-hole digger are propped precariously in a corner just to the left of the living room door. Gravity causes the tools to slip inexorably downward, until eventually they stick into the living room doorway and waylay unsuspecting visitors.

This accumulation didn't begin as actual hoarding. According to Merriam-Webster, hoarding is *the compulsion to continually accumu-*

late a variety of items that are often considered useless or worthless by others accompanied by an inability to discard the items without great distress. The accumulation in the mudroom was more rational, an outcome of living on limited means a long way from town, where every bucket and tin can that could hold any might-come-in-handy screw, bolt, nut, nail, or sawed-off piece of pipe was saved. As for me, I know that I'm not a true hoarder because eventually the clutter absolutely pisses me off.

Part of the human condition includes a near limitless capacity for getting used to oppressive relationships of all kinds: annoying commutes, barking dogs, worn-out walking shoes, bad habits in ourselves and others, and most recently those damned masks that obscure our breathing and facial expressions. Until today, I have negotiated this mess in the mudroom and managed to find what I needed. But this first October of my retirement, this month when all hell was breaking loose on every front, this year where it seemed like the only orderly thing was the odd symmetry of the numbers 2020, I finally hit the wall with the mess in the mudroom. The breaking point came two weeks ago when the floor was so cluttered with crap that the door from the front porch wouldn't open all the way. Kim tripped over my chainsaw in the living room. It was there because I had no other place to put it. She pled her case. I shriveled; my inner Gollum that had been slapping along in his slippery cave for years came fully into the brightness of the fall day.

So I began. I committed to declutter everything to the right of the door. Large items were dragged into the yard. I propped open a heavy-duty contractor garbage bag and began stuffing it with rolls of linoleum and tubes of petrified adhesives. A wooden fruit box became the metal recycling bin. The box soon sprouted with plumbing parts, towel racks, various hardware, and a toilet paper dispenser. Decaying lawn chairs shedding particles of nylon were carried gingerly to a growing pile of refuse outside. I grabbed my COVID mask from the truck and swept up archival rodent turds and dust. The shop vacuum inhaled more dust, droppings, spider webs, and a few unfortunate spiders who weren't speedy enough to escape the ruthless vortex of the nozzle that nosed over floors and walls.

Faced with a shit pile like this, Marie Kondo would likely run screaming into the brushy hills. I wasn't about to ask whether a can of rusty nails bent like brown arthritic fingers brought me joy. Instead, I repeated the mantra of my neighbor up the road who was helping clean out a friend's intergenerational accumulation: *this was once useful here, and now it needs to find another use in a different place.* In other words, it needed to find its way to a metal shredder, be melted in the crucible of a furnace, formed into bars, and finally shipped away and used in any of millions of metal-containing products. Not only would the mudroom become more tolerable, perhaps even useful, the process was saving vast amounts of virgin metals and energy. And even though I hate filling up our limited landfills, at least the rest of the garbage would be compacted and isolated, not to mention somewhere else. The only joy to be found here was in a bare floor. The chainsaw could return to the mudroom. Kim would smile.

When the family arrived to press cider on the following day, Kim didn't just smile. She beamed like a ripe autumn apple. Even though I had managed to declutter only one side of the room, even though it still smelled like woodrat piss, at least there was room to inhale. The open space allowed my chest to expand a little more with each breath. Did my contentment qualify as a muted version of joy? Who cares. In this time when joy seems to have become a rare coin in the currency of the world, I'll take contentment to the bank.

Maybe sometime in the next ten years I'll clean out the other side.

19. Post and Beam

I live in the most beautiful place in the world. Even on this murky October afternoon that swells like a gray inhalation, even when darkening valleys hold their breath and keep their secrets close, even when the ecstasy of vine maple colors are keeping to themselves, even when the clearcuts seem especially bruised, even in this year of COVID that continues to carom along the infinite tracks of time. Even in all of this droop and drab, my tiny slice of the universe is the most beautiful place I know. Because I know it.

The pickup makes a tight U-turn in the parking area of the Johnny Gunter place on Upper Smith River. Clouds string apart into sun-warmed taffy, and I peel down to a tattered T-shirt. The meadow swirls with the acrid aroma of apple cider vinegar. Our family Cider Day was five days ago when four generations reduced untold boxes of apples to 35 gallons of cider. Two hundred pounds of pressed apple leavings were piled beside the snowball bush. This afternoon only a thin layer of fermented mush remains, inscribed with the hand-sized track of a young bear. In the greening grass ten feet from the apple heap lie two softball-size piles of bear poop. These are identical in color and texture to the original pile. I laugh. In my mind I see the bloated bear squatting in the yard, too full to waddle any further from the pile. I hope our leavings still contain enough nutrition for the bear to put on a little more fat going into winter.

Today I'm here to build a shelter for a shared portable sawmill now residing at my co-owner's place near Eugene. This fall, he and I will move the mill to the house in the Coast Range. To prepare for that day, all spring and summer I've hauled small logs from storm-damaged trees at the Johnny Gunter place to the mill an hour away in town. I've sawed those logs into lumber and then trucked the boards back to the old house, where they are stacked and waiting to be assembled into the shelter.

The ruthless metric of efficiency cries out against this back-and-forth movement of wood. But living consciously isn't always efficient. For the past year I've been having conversations with the house and the trees. Talking with trees and houses in the current heave of human-caused chaos can be both sobering and settling. These exchanges also take time, both to learn the right questions and to hear the answers. In the end, I'm honoring my agreement with the house and trees to use only wood from this property for the project.

From inside the mudroom I retrieve a handful of carpentry tools: pencil, hammer, level, square, and a circular saw. The tools are rudimentary and match my level of skill. I press those once downed trees back to verticality as blonde 4 × 4s. They are held in place by pier blocks with brackets rather than by roots and stabilized on top by 2 × 8 beams instead of branches. I stop often to stare at the rising structure. My body learns by doing, and everything needs to be done at least twice. This clumsy exercise against entropy is always in all ways inefficient.

Posts and beams have been raised when the sun-blanched afternoon thickens into evening. Daylight slides away toward winter. Moonless darkness freezes time in its tracks, forcing me to stop. Mars gleams in the southeast like the distant eye of Sauron.

On the front porch, I strap on a headlamp. Diffuse light spreads to the back of the meadow, where three pairs of eyes gleam like bright planets. The doe and her twin yearlings have bedded. On Cider Day they wandered through the open orchard gate and were happily browsing the apple foliage. My daughter and I encouraged them to leave. This was traumatic for them, but they seem to have forgiven me (if a deer's brain contains the capacity for forgiveness). Probably they are only bulging and burping from a large helping of fermented apple mash. I wonder if they are sober.

Occasionally I misspeak and say that I come to this place to escape. In fact, I come here to drop anchor, moored by deer and bears who feast on the leftovers of a century of intergenerational cider-making in this valley. I come here to be held together by trees. Some of them are dead and brought into another life with screws and nails as shelter from the rain. But most are still living, their boughs speaking the sighing sentences of an incoming storm. In these tumultuous days at the end of the life we thought we knew, I wish everyone could say they live in the most beautiful place in the world. Because there are many most beautiful places in the world. There are as many of those places as people who are willing to know them in that soulful way that says *This is who I am; this is how I live.*

20. Frost

In years past I've been too busy to pull out the summer garden before the first killing frost. Things have changed. I've left my job and retired into a covidian freefall. This fall I've decided to avoid the inevitable November postmortem mess of frost-blackened tomato and squash plants and opted for a mercy killing. At the Johnny Gunter place, I clip honey-skinned butternut squash with pruning loppers, snap off a few hopeful zucchinis sprouting like dark green sausages, grab any tomato with a chance of ripening, and chuck the green ones over the garden fence to feed the untamed. I finish with a final flush of aromatherapy by burying my face in basil leaves. Autumn squash roots always surprise me, the secret subterranean spread of entrails inside a dark abdomen. Within one hour all that was once vibrant and lush, all that inhaled springwater and carbon dioxide, all that exhaled oxygen and food for my family is piled in the corner of the garden in a pyre of decomposition. The suddenness of eradication creates a tight place in the space between my heart and throat.

I rattle the pickup and trailer up a gravel road to the ridgetop. I'll fill the trailer from a pile of wood chips, the remains of tree limbs and tops cut while clearing a new logging road. The chips will be spread around the sawmill to keep the mud at bay when milling begins this winter. At the chip pile, cool and unsettling wind stirs wispy clouds. My biceps strain under the shovel, but I don't break a sweat before the trailer is full. The pickup and I twist back along the ridge where transient phone service comes and goes. There is a text from my wife. COVID has struck close to home, causing a brief wave of anxiety. I call her. I'm pissed off. Fear sometimes makes me angry.

Back at the sawmill site, I spread most of the chips and pile the rest for later. A cold and cloudless dusk settles over my shoulders. Moon is a crescent chased by Jupiter along the southern ridge while Saturn looks on. I sit on the darkening porch with a bowl of warmed-up pasta. Forty-two degrees. Frost on the way.

Summer cricket buzz is reduced to a final act. A duet. From the far end of the meadow, one voice is a pulsing murmur that rises and falls like the breathing of a person deep in sleep. The other is a soft monotonic chitter from the orchard behind me, like a Douglas squirrel with laryngitis. I'm not certain whether they are different species. Regardless, neither insect will survive the night. I think of "The Last Cricket" by Steve Edwards, an essay on waiting for the end of the final cricket song of the year. The waning cricket music is how I imagine arriving fully conscious to the moment of my death.

A few cold-weather chores are waiting in the house: wash my dinner bowl, drain the pipes, remove the filter from the kitchen faucet, pack up the old laptop computer. I return to the porch. A shard of moon, clear-eyed and intense, throws my shadow onto the weathered shingles.

The crickets are silent.

21. Whole

Early November darkness. I'm chilled from working into cold dusk on a shelter for the portable mill, an early step on the road to rehabilitating this old house in the Coast Range. I am newly retired from a career as a gene jockey in which I manipulated invisible things in small tubes. Now I'm learning to build structures that I can bang my head against. "Learning" is a process in which half my carpentry must be redone and half of what is redone must be re-redone. This evening, my learning process has been mercifully terminated by nightfall. Inside the house, I settle my beat-up body into a beat-up chair next to the woodstove. After a week of electoral mayhem, several months of overt racial turmoil, and half a year watching my fellow humans struggle against a viral particle 0.1 microns in size with a propensity for killing people, this evening my connections to the wider world are pared down to this: the warming mumble of a fire, a lamp over my right shoulder that casts the living room in half-light, that familiar metronomic *cluck* of the wall clock, a black pen, and my journal.

Somewhere I read that writers aren't supposed to write about their writing. Where do all these damned rules come from? I've done my level best to find words that drill down to some core that describes the heartwood of us all, a fundamental humanity that defies our superficial differences. Writer activists whom I respect have lobbied me to join in the cultural fray. As a grandfather in a newly interracial family, you'd think I'd dive right in. But I'm more interested in exploring avenues along which we can move toward a unified future, one in which my descendants might live whole and uncompromised lives. If you're wondering whether I have opinions, I do. Strong ones. As in more than one. But most are trivial compared with the larger whole I'm trying to puzzle together.

Wholeness is dynamic. It fluctuates in the way our body temperature oscillates around 98.6 degrees. Words don't seem adequate to explain the wholeness I feel in this small valley in the hills, removed from many things I love.

In this dark November silence, I feel complete, even though the fullness of my existence requires separation from the chaos of the past week. Here there is no talking-head cable TV. No Red. No Blue. No bullshit. The woodstove asks very little of me in our two-way conversation, only an occasional stick of wood from the front porch. When I return to town I'll become whole in other ways that include my family and neighborhood.

I have very little with which to chart a path toward healing. My intuition, my heart, a little blind faith. Maybe it doesn't matter. The stove needs feeding, though. I'll step out and grab another piece of wood. Pull up your chair in this half-light shouldering into the season of darkness, the season of gratitude. Reach out your hands. The stove will burn into the unbroken night. Listen to the warmth. Feel the drum of rain on the metal roof. But remember—the house will be cold by morning.

22. Roof

Early afternoon in late November. The pickup and I were bending into the convolutions of a logging road on the way to the Johnny Gunter place. "Partly sunny" hadn't materialized. An overcast sky embraced the hills like an animal breathing heavily, exhaling foggy wraiths onto needled ridges. For two weeks I'd been poised to finish the roof on the mill shed I've been building. Plans sometimes change quickly. Thanksgiving came early when a grouse and I crossed paths. This was the end of the grouse's life as it had known it but dinner for me.

Filet of grouse deserved a pile of chanterelles. In the afternoon gloom, I stepped away from the roofing project and plied the old forest behind the house for fungi. My expectation of silence was shredded by a gaggle of voices reaching into the big trees from my right. A group of kids unleashed a volley of hollering and fake hooting that brought some feral impulse welling into my throat. I slipped deeper into the shadows, away from their exuberance. For a few moments, the prospect of winter hardened in my chest like the chill of gray basalt. I rested my shoulder against an ancient Douglas-fir. Blinked into the depth of the dying day. Found some easy breaths. The stone in my chest softened. Somehow I managed to embrace all of it, the intrusive voices, the ominous afternoon, the impending season of darkness. In the process, I stumbled into a small patch of chanterelles that gifted me just enough mushrooms for dinner. Then the moonless night closed over all of us, soft and dark and complete as death.

In the morning I was back on task and up on the ladder. Tepid sunlight shouldered through thin overcast while I fastened 1 × 4 crosspieces along the tops of the rafters. The rough-cut lumber bristled with a layer of thin blond fur, a winter coat for the coming dark times. When all of the crosspieces were fastened down, I sorted through a stack of corrugated green metal roofing and several bags of roofing screws, leftovers from when Dad roofed the house and garage twenty years ago. I slid six sheets up onto the finished frame of the roof, each one overlapping by a single ridge. I have trust issues with my carpentry;

setting the ladder, I took a deep breath and climbed onto the roof to start driving screws. The frame held.

I have erected this shed alone, a project that has been the antithesis of an Amish barn raising. My reasons for going solo are more complex than just an arcane need to create balance in the universe. My isolation was imposed in part by a viral pandemic. There were also idiosyncratic motives: my craving for quiet headspace, some embarrassment around my bumbling carpentry, and a kinesthetic need to learn things with my body rather than watching someone else (this strategy is especially effective when everything must be done twice!).

I work alone also because I'm my father's son. I've been thinking of Dad a lot during this project. I have the memory of him late in his life sitting across the table telling me that he would never ask for help unless he absolutely needed it. I love my father and am grateful for most of what he gave me. But I'll spend the rest of my living days unlearning this false sense of independence. The roofing for the mill shelter is here because of Dad. The property is here because Uncle Johnny kept it in the family. The mill and power tools are here because of an unfathomable complexity of supply chains. The trees are here because of the myriad geological and biological factors that came together to grow a forest. The only solo aspect of this first building project has been my own muscles, and today even these were fueled by a grouse and some chanterelles, gifts from the forest.

Three p.m. The last roofing screw wormed its way into metal and wood. A windless overcast thickened quietly from the west, obliterating the insipid sun. I backed the ladder a few steps away from the shed and climbed it to gain a little height for some pictures. The rain began on cue. A smatter of tentative ticks peppered the new roof. These were quickly transformed into a density of descending water. From inside the shelter I listened to the hammer of deluge meeting metal, grateful to be dry. Life in an apocalypse seemed inordinately good.

23. Dinner

How dinner happens in the kitchen of our suburban homestead:

Take grandsons to the park for the afternoon. Drive them back to their house across town. On the drive home remember you didn't plan dinner. Wonder why are you so damned tired and only want to get home, mix drinks, and collapse. Arrive home. Mix drinks. Fall into easy chairs. Enjoy that first happy flush of ethanol.

Hunger drives you out. Quick shopping trip to storage freezer in garage. Find package of Open Nature No Antibiotics Ever Roasted Red Pepper and Garlic Chicken Sausages. Ignore ingredients list outing them as a product of Lucerne Foods, Inc. They were on sale. Defrost in microwave, miracle machine invented by Gods of the Unplanned.

Wander into front garden. Dusk drops like a wet stone. Pick endive, kale, chicory, and corn salad planted last August. Be smug you had the foresight to plant seeds in time for winter greens. Hand greens to life partner who insists on hand-shredding to maximize adherence of salad dressing. Don't call bullshit.

Instead, slice up precooked Johnny Gunter potatoes for skillet fries. Stumble into backyard for a leek. Slice that, too. Get leek cooking in a skillet with olive oil. Add sliced potatoes. Have another swig of whatever is still out on the counter. Return to backyard. It's now dark as a bear's ass in hibernation. Pick parsley, sage, and oregano by braille. Chop herbs. Add to potatoes and leeks. The mix seems dry. Throw in more olive oil.

Retrieve now-thawed corporate No-Antibiotics-Ever sausages from microwave. Chuck them into yet another pan knowing it won't be washed until morning. Brown on all sides. Find jar of homemade sauerkraut. Find jar of lactic-acid-fermented summer vegetables that includes Oregon Giant beans, carrots, beets, and potato onions. Congratulate self for having grown all that shit. Throw sausage package into garbage bin so that you'll never have to see it again.

Pour wine from a bottle opened three days ago. Sit down. Enjoy.

24. Bench

COVID sucks. I'm tired of being physically disconnected from my various tribes, tired of digital half-heartedness, tired of having heartfelt connections with no physical space in which to manifest them. No hugs. No handshakes. No hamburgers and beers with friends. I'm sick of it, but fortunately not yet sick.

Late November rain is taking a breather. Because chanterelle picking is both socially and physically distant, I drive into the coastal mountains to hunt for mushrooms and some peace of mind. Or is it a piece of mind? At times I feel as if I own this glistening road draped across the ridgetops like a black snake. It winds along the edge of my world, tracing the irregular edges of life as I've come to know it. Winter solstice is creeping up. Her unseen arms reach from below the southern horizon and pull Sun relentlessly downward, drawing evergreen shadows across wet asphalt.

A wide spot appears on my right. I pull over because it is an easy place to stop. My mushroom basket is in the back. Stepping off the familiar edge of a road in this precipitous country is a commitment to letting go—a downhill plunge away from human-made security into contorted vine maple, swishing sword fern, and a tripping tumble of blackberry brambles. In the Coast Range, stepping off a road is an embrace of all things that thrive in darkness.

I make a short descent to a bench covered with thirty-year-old second-growth trees. There should be chanterelles here, but the mushrooms have long since been picked. I'm too close to the safety of the road. Leaving the bench, I continue my downhill plunge knowing that to haul my sixty-plus-year-old body back to the pickup I'll fight gravity on a slope steep as an elk's ass. Second-growth Douglas-fir unexpectedly relinquishes the slope to uncut native forest. An abruptness of overstory presses skyward on giant hemlock and fir trunks. The understory thins, and I can see another wide bench about one hundred yards below me. There aren't any chanterelles here either, but I'm drawn to this untouched place. In the Coast Range, only 7% of the original forest remains, and that's a generous estimate.

In this landscape of steep canyons and narrow ridges, the confluence of big trees and level places is as rare as grouse teeth.

Life-giving death greets me on the old-growth bench. A rotten stump is scattered with the wet feathers of an unfortunate grouse, probably now being digested by a Cooper's hawk or great-horned owl. Decay is everywhere. Logs reduced to red rot are growing huckleberry and salal. A Douglas-fir log four feet in diameter stretches prone before me, corrugated bark filled with moss that nurses the roots of baby hemlock trees. Stillness is disrupted by a furtive movement in the root-wad of the toppled fir. Douglas Squirrel clings to a root, holds me with dark agate eyes, then vanishes into a silence of sword ferns and trees who have nothing and everything to say.

I spread my arms wide trying to grasp tens of millions of years, the layered accumulation of a place. But my reach is too small. For reference, I have only the span of my life and the inconvenience of a COVID year of disrupted routines. New Year's Day is coming. Raise a toast, because right now we need any excuse for amusement. But remember that the measure of our year means nothing. The world that contains our lives will not magically change when the odometer on the Gregorian calendar turns over. If such a thing as time exists, it is marked by the daily turn of Earth and solstice Sun sagging over these mountains as they rose from the sea. By Moon driving tides and waves that cut sandstone into level places that would someday host old trees and the small silent eyes of squirrels. By the reaching arms of a human trying to gain a handhold of consciousness in deepening shadows. The infinity of time cares not a whit about arbitrary constructs of human seconds and minutes.

The time to live has always been now. The time to die has always been then. From within this moment, I choose life. All of it. Mumbling a small thank you, I drop my arms, pick up the empty mushroom basket, and sweat my way back to the security of the road.

25. EVERGREEN

The morning sky is two dimensional, nameless. At midday we name it Downpour. Cloud-Water-Descending. Incessant. I'm behind the wheel of Dad's old crew cab Ford pickup, a blue and silver leviathan nosing through the deluge. Daughter Laurel and wife Kim join me in the prodigious front seat. From the rear seat, our two grandsons watch the gray-green sea of mountains slide past steamed-up windows. The pickup is the antithesis of my little Nissan, which has a turning radius the diameter of a squirrel's sphincter. Still, I am oddly comfortable piloting this behemoth. Dad has been gone nearly three years, but there seems to be some uniquely Titus-shaped space that gathers me into the driver's seat. Dad's sweat is in the upholstery. His calloused hands are still on the wheel. The road coils into me through his eyes. At the Johnny Gunter place, the pickup squishes into rivulets of runoff flowing down each rut in the driveway. I stop to unlock the gate. On cue, the boys scramble out of the cab and settle their small butts onto the rain-soaked floor of the pickup bed for their customary open-air ride to the house. Opportunities for wetness abound.

We find the small evergreen on the edge of the old forest, edge of shadow, edge of maximum darkness, edge of its demise at the hands of our holiday. Thin needles are predecorated with strands of gray beard lichen sent down from the Old Ones. Chris watches with big eyes while Laurel helps Edmund with the bowsaw in the way I once helped her. The tree shudders and finally falls. His small seven-year-old voice yells *TIMBER!!* He knows what to yell when a tree dies. How will I teach him to celebrate when a tree lives on? I realize that I have forgotten to ask for permission from the mountains to take the tree away. This oversight bothers me, especially in this tumultuous year when so many humans have died, and the value of life in its multitude of forms has been discounted. Asking does not always result in a clear answer, but the question always matters.

Across the valley, the skinhead top of a clearcut mountain blooms like Mt. Doom. Orange petals of flame unfurl into the ash-colored sky, a conflagration of forest leftovers piled after the cutting. The loggers probably didn't ask permission either. My gaze keeps flying to the fire like a wide-eyed winter moth. I wonder how many wet seasons our house might have been warmed if that explosion of heat been doled out slowly in the controlled burn of our woodstove.

We carry the skinny tree down a deer trail veined with muddy water trickling toward the heart of the valley. One more task remains. Kim herds everyone toward the orchard while I grab a shovel from the house. We push open the pipe-frame gate. A 12-inch Douglas-fir reaches hopefully through the woven wire fencing. It is a descendent of the old forest and has no future where it has rooted. After a slicing scoop into rain-soaked soil, the little tree is riding on the shovel blade to a new home, roots dangling like worms through the dark earth. We carry the seedling to the edge of the forest that spawned it, where a phalanx of young firs is already marching relentlessly into the meadow. I stab open the ground and slide the infant tree's roots into the wound, tendrils carrying their child's gift of orchard soil and microbes. The seedling is tamped gently upright, our tribute to the life we just took and a future of biological succession that will supersede all of us. Someday someone will fertilize this tree with my ashes.

Back at the parking area the boys and I celebrate our wildness by stamping through water-filled ruts. On the front porch, Kim helps the kids peel off their soaking clothes as rain exclaims on the metal roof. I hang dripping pants, ponder the miracle of trees. I run aground on the deep and messy questions of human existence. Like *how can a kid fill up his rubber boots in only two inches of water?*

26. Conversations

Three days after Christmas, the sawmill was moved to the Johnny Gunter place. Although the mill is "portable," the move took most of the day. My co-owner and I needed his lift-bucket tractor and small SUV, Dad's enormous pickup, and a hand winch. My daughter Laurel and her guy Ethan threw their young bodies into the fray. Even with their youthful enthusiasm I expended a lot of old-guy sounds and well-placed cuss words. With nightfall rising from the ground like dark water, the mill was finally positioned beneath the new shelter, stretched like an orange robot queen on her day bed. We christened the first log with a splash of beer, made one cut by the light of our headlamps, and called it a day.

Now for the hard stuff. Here on the leading edge of a new year, the current of time is dragging us flailing into an uncertain future. People are out of work, isolated, pissed off, oppressed, lonely, afraid, and dying in increasing numbers. Me? One or two of those adjectives might apply, but mostly the word *fortunate* only begins to describe my life. While much of the world has devolved into pandemic turmoil, I have the outrageously good fortune of contemplating a sawmill and a worthy project. The mill is here to make lumber for mending the old house that was built from rough-cut boards milled by my maternal great-uncle Johnny and framed with the carpentry skills of my paternal grandfather Roland.

There is a sweet continuity in knowing that lumber milled by me will be used to fix a house built from lumber milled by Johnny. Yet I also carry a burden of responsibility. Owning a sawmill makes one acutely aware that lumber comes from trees. A few logs are already lined up in the parking area. Some of these came from a Douglas-fir that was casting too much shade on the garden. The others are from trees damaged by the heavy snow of 2019. But the project will require about 250 boards and battens and an unknown quantity of other lumber to replace rotten parts in the frame. Milling that lumber will require more trees—not a lot of trees, but more than have been cut so far. These trees are long-time residents on a piece of the Earth I have come to know intimately. This intimacy has led to an awareness that they are living participants in a dynamic ecosystem that will carry on long after my body has been reduced to molecular bits and pieces of forest soil.

My relationship with these trees could be very simple. I could just cut them down. I'm pretty good with a chainsaw and have the "freedom" to do any damned thing I want with it on this property. But freedom functions only within the larger context of community, which in this case is a forest. But even "forest" is a cumulative abstraction that depersonalizes the individuals within it. I need to cut individual trees. If I don't already have a relationship with them, I soon will, even if only in the intimacy of death.

If taken seriously, these connections can become a little overwhelming. So I have been asking for permission to take those who are needed. On some days (and occasionally at night), I speak out loud while walking the small property. Other times I sit in dank duff beneath the dark drip of closed overstory and let my mind spin silently. Trees speak among themselves in a language of airborne hormones and chemicals transported through roots connected by fungal intermediaries. Their words are not directly accessible to me. But I listen anyway because I have my intuition, that fascinating combination of emotion, familiarity, and acute attentiveness. Intuition is often referred to as a "gut-level" response. For me it seems to be lodged in my chest, somewhere in the vicinity of my heart, a place where feelings supersede language.

Answers have emerged from these conversations. Some are rules: leave no direct sunlight drying the forest floor, minimize disruption to the duff, maintain the interconnection of roots, leave the oldest ones to become Older Ones, replace every tree taken by transplanting a seedling to the edge of the meadow, and by all means take only what is needed. Some of these insights are gifts of individual trees: one above the meadow is half-dead from drought, another at the edge of the forest bleeds black from a fungal infection, and I recently discovered a pocket of storm-damaged trees above the driveway. In time there might be others.

Sometimes my science mind intervenes in these discussions. *Have I made all this shit up in my head?* Partially, I suppose. But hard-edged rationality seems like a cheap argument. Intuition doesn't materialize in a vacuum. It requires knowledge and attentiveness. Intuition leads to relevant questions. Answers might be forthcoming, but the questioner must be listening. Understanding is contingent upon a shared language. In this small parcel of forest tucked within the pleated green of canyon and ridge, that language is borne on microbes and mosses, sword ferns and salamanders, and the way Sun bends his way through evergreen branches and splashes across wet needle rot. The trees will have their say. I will listen inside my chest.

27. OLD PICKUP

An unusually dry January afternoon lies in parallel planes of blue and gray. No sun dazzle. No wild-eyed blue. No drama. Sky has simply grown tired of raining and is resting on her couch. Her cloud lines run strangely parallel in contour and color to the old pickup stretched like a blue whale calf beached on my concrete driveway, its hood and cab peeling clear-coat like a sunburn.

When Dad died nearly three years ago, he left many things behind, animate and otherwise. One of these was this 1995 Ford F-350 diesel dual cab. It was a replacement for a similar pickup. He wrecked that one at the foot of his driveway while trying to turn left off the highway with his bulldozer on a flatbed trailer pushing hard from behind. Mass, inertia, and the ineluctable laws of physics drove him into a utility pole. Mostly though, Dad took excellent care of his vehicles until the last several years of his life. Then the ravages of Parkinson's disease eventually made putting on his weather-beaten Carhartt jacket difficult.

Recently, I've taken on the task of catching up on deferred maintenance for this old truck. I changed the oil, oil filter, and fuel filter and had the transmission serviced. Air conditioning pump, alternator, and serpentine belt were replaced. Power steering fluid was flushed. This week I drove the truck over the mountains to my brother's shop so he could help me replace the brake pads and shoes. We spent the day spitting curses onto rusty recalcitrant iron like pissed-off camels. This seemed to help.

The pickup project was born in pragmatism, or at least what passes for pragmatism in my life. My pickup is a small two-wheel drive, and I needed something with more traction and oomph to pull logs to the portable sawmill to cut lumber for breathing new life into the Johnny Gunter house. Generally speaking, I'm not into inanimate things. I became a biologist because I'm attracted to living organisms. But Dad's truck has taken on aspects of a living being.

I use the term "living" advisedly. Today, a carpet vacuum screams while I work the soapy lather from an upholstery attachment over the truck's filthy floor and seat covers. The vacuum inhales muddy suds from the driver's side floor. Short white dog hairs are exhumed from the passenger and rear seat upholstery. Pepper was a good dog. She was conceived when someone turned their back on my brother's registered German shorthaired pointer who was in heat, and she quickly found a blue heeler consort. Pepper was born in a camper on an extended family camping trip to Dad's childhood stomping grounds above Hells Canyon. She was the Unchosen of a giveaway mongrel litter and came to live with Mom and Dad. In those first years after my family and I returned to Oregon, Pepper always greeted us with a happy woof and wag in their driveway. Years after she died, I still expected her welcome. A shiver of loss runs through me watching her hair disappear into the wailing vacuum.

I could sequence Pepper's admixed genome from those hairs. I could sequence Dad's genome from his skin cells sucked from the upholstery. A genome is only a complex blueprint for a life, not the life itself, and I wouldn't know Pepper or Dad, even from the totality of their DNA. And yet the old pickup contains the genetic essence of those no longer with us. It also carries Dad's grinning great-grandsons riding in the back up the driveway to the Johnny Gunter house his father helped to build. The old pickup pulls logs that will become living lumber for keeping that house standing for another generation. The old pickup blends dog hair and skin cells and sweat and relationships and memories of the living with those who are gone.

We cannot discern where any dad or dog or pickup begins or ends in space or time. Fuzzy edges are the nature of all individual things, living or not. An old pickup can blur the lines separating those who are breathing from those who breathe no longer. How ironic that we as a society now suffer mightily from false partitions erected among us, aided and abetted by corporate media and politicians of all stripes. Why then do we, who are unquestionably alive, who belong to the same biological species, and who are gathered into a common geopolitical entity, seem hell-bent on raising impenetrable walls among us? Maybe we need a little hair of the dog. Or a project disguised as something practical. Maybe we need a return to some sort of common memory.

28. Precarious

At the edge of the continent at the edge of normal, a Sitka spruce clings precariously from a wave-crashed cliff. The spruce is small but not young. Needled fingers implore the sepia sunset for one more day. Just one more day above this crescent moon beach of crushed shells, of kelp no longer holding fast, of frayed and wooly drift logs ravaged by beach stones. The stones are smooth, gentling in the curl of my hand.

Tomorrow the highway going north will be closed. On that stretch where it loops like licorice rope around basalt headlands, a piece of pavement slides toward the gaping ocean. Again. As if the road knows by rite of gravity and flush of late winter rain where it belongs. More rebar, more asphalt, more human energy devoted to hanging on. Maybe just for one more day.

Eighty or so sanderlings and I follow lines of cloud, sand, and surf. Our similarities end here. Their short black legs churn in unison with one another, a choreographed flock of baseball-size bodies dancing with incoming waves. I'm solitary, with legs long and loping and pale. One bird dives exuberantly into the surf, needle beak churning the spreading saltwater. Ten others follow her. I keep my white running shoes dry by jogging diagonally to incoming waves. I love the way sanderlings exploit this narrow space that separates the safety of our landed lives from certain death in a cold ocean.

Circling of predators. Bald eagle hovers osprey-like above the surf. Waiting. Waiting. Diving. Talons spread and plunge into surging water and emerge wet and empty. A fisherman stands waist-deep in waves, casting baited hooks. His bag is empty. The dark driftwood head of a sea lion bobs twenty yards offshore. Is her stomach empty? A cluster of food fish has likely drawn everyone together, all of these fervent and unrelinquishing eaters and eaten. All of this ebb and flow.

High tide line is littered with sea jellies. Some are ten translucent inches in diameter, every one of them long since dead. Did they die at sea and wash up postmortem? Or did they cluster in this same parcel of the Pacific where fisher and sea lion and bald eagle now search for sustenance, only to be cast ashore in the regurgitation of a storm? An infinite gulf of dry sand separates their ignominious decomposition from churning waves on which they so gracefully drifted. I cannot step on them.

This precarious edge. A continent battered by storms slides submissively over the Pacific Plate that carries an ocean floor into the center of the earth. On the way down, it may snag and cause the big hiccup of a subduction earthquake. It might descend smoothly, become molten, emerge fiery from an inland volcano, and cool to rock and soil that subtend a forest. This flux of tide and passion is where humans persist with highways and hotels, where small birds swing to and fro, where fish and fishers swirl together. Waves thin as window glass separate the living from the dead-but-about-to-live-again-in-another-form. Life tips on edge, trying to fit. Just one more day.

29. Relationships

In January I was compelled to go winter steelhead fishing on the North Fork of Smith River. But the Coast Range was still gushing gravity-driven water from every gash and pore, and the water in the stream was too high. I thrashed my way in heavy waders through prickly salmonberry canes and tripping vine maple. I was feeling stretched as thin as those conifer-caught clouds that couldn't quite clear the ridge. My plan had been to spend the night in the pickup canopy, a little scrunched but dry. I'm not an accomplished steelhead fisher even under the best of circumstances. So I chose to abort the mission and swam back upstream by driving the entirety of Smith River Road to the Johnny Gunter place. There I would find a woodstove, electric lights, hot dinner, bourbon, and a bed.

This is a long drive any time of the year. But in midwinter the trip can be an adventure. Jeffrey Foucault's lyrics poured fast and loud from the speakers. *IT'S TOO LATE TO GO HOME EARLY ANYMORE* ... I sang along at high volume as crystal curtains of runoff leapt hell-bent over roadside cliffs. Smith River Falls was a muddy torrent plunging the eroded skeleton of the mountains toward the sea. With many miles to go, darkness chased the pickup down. I was engulfed by a black esophagus of asphalt that carried me ever deeper into the guts of the mountains. Broken bodies of trees were stretched prone across the road. Large impetuous raindrops pummeled the cab and bounced from glistening pavement into my headlights like little incandescent frogs. Just when it seemed I was running out of steam on this inclement adventure, the driveway was there, slanting hard uphill to the left. Rarely have I been happier to unlock that gate, get into the house, and build a fire. Culinary expediency called for canned chili and instant mashed potatoes for dinner. Rain hammered the metal roof, beating me into a warm and senseless sleep.

Silence roared in on the dawn. Thirty-four-degree daylight sifted over a tentative skiff of snow on the meadow. Conifers drooped under their midwinter weariness of slush. Moon hung half-full in a blue window of sky framed by clouds, becoming translucent as she relinquished the night sky to Sun. In the living room, the woodstove grumbled with the effort of keeping the drafty house warm.

This was pruning season, but I was in no hurry to go to work on fruit trees still clinging to shawls of sloppy wet snow. Instead, I pulled an old chair up to the stove and read a short Barry Lopez essay, "Children in the Woods" from his collection *Crossing Open Ground*. In 1982 Lopez was, as usual, far ahead of his time. He recognized that the most important gift we can give kids in wild spaces is a heart sense of relationship rather than the mindy minutiae of names and facts. Barry describes a deeper experience of the living world that can be found by expanding a specific instance such as finding a raccoon jaw to include all the relationships, including those of humans, that nestled the bone into that place at that time.

The warmth of Barry's words mingled with heat from the woodstove and radiated into my chest. Within the context of the natural world, he gave credence to an idea I've championed for years—that the job of raising kids, the job for all of us who continue to grow up and grow older, is to become less self-centered, more inclusive. We can measure the quality of our lives to the extent that we become invested in our connections with others, our investment in all beings, human or not, animate or not. This change in perspective has become a life-long personal process. My family heritage is a merging of twin streams of maternal and paternal independence. Men were reared on an up-by-your-bootstraps mythology and were taught that interdependence is a weakness. This familial culture challenges me to live more inclusively. Sometimes I succeed in realizing a wider vision for people and the world. Then an even deeper complication kicks in. I'm fundamentally an introvert and need solitude to recharge my personal battery.

Humans are the outcome of many formative forces, including our evolutionary past. We are the living story of a 2.5-billion-year history of life driven by the need for individual survival. Only for the last 50 million years of our primate ancestry has survival been predicated on the need for belonging to a group.

No wonder we are so easily swayed by the purveyors of self-serving, individual freedoms at the expense of the full flower of interrelatedness within which we actually exist. No wonder we are in constant conflict between self-centered desire and meeting the needs of others. And yet I wonder. Might we focus on that eye-blink of the last 50 million years and embrace our relationships? Could we look past our momentary desires and into the eyes of our children and grandchildren who will walk into the future long after we have stepped aside and abandoned the trail of life? Please. Show me the wisdom contained in a raccoon jaw.

30. Bones

Earlier in the week, my bones felt unusually anxious. I'm a little high strung, but generalized anxiety isn't usually my jam. Yet I couldn't ignore that amorphous troglodyte rising from the dark caverns of my marrow, its cold fingers groping the space beneath my sternum, searching for my heart. My heart tried to run but was trapped. My heart needed me to speak the nameless into the light, but I had no voice. I thought a nap would help. But when I woke, the anxiety continued to circle a racetrack in my chest. Sometimes an apocalypse can do that.

My bones needed an infusion of unfiltered spring water. Uncounted weeks had passed since I visited that quiet space in the Coast Range, a room-size basin where forest water burbles into dim light. With evening light making its gentle transit toward nightfall, I walked up the easy slope to the spring and was greeted by a thin slice of chaos. A recent storm had toppled an old Douglas-fir, who in her rush to the ground had broken off a bigleaf maple twenty feet up. A compound fracture of bared wood stabbed a new gash into the canopy, bleeding fading daylight onto sword ferns.

This brief violence of falling wood had tipped my drinking cup from its resting place on an old brick, casting it into the two-gallon pool where water gathers for its trip to the valley floor. I retrieved the cup, polished the accumulated minerals from white ceramic, dip, and drank in cold steady pulls. From the pool I scooped out a crumble of sandstone, the broken bones of these mountains. Pebble grit, slippery mud, and aching water impregnated the skin of my bare hand, breaching the partition between my inner and my outer. Dissolved rock percolated into my bones, bearing witness against any illusion of separateness.

A burrow four inches in diameter was bored into the slope above the seep. In front of the burrow was an orderly stack of lanceolate fern fronds, their snipped stems gathered and pointing together into the hole. A mountain beaver is a rodent that isn't a beaver. Some folks call it a boomer, except that it doesn't boom either. I can't remember how I know that this excavation and fern harvest are the doings of a mountain beaver. At this point in my life, some things just are.

Sunset. Back on the porch. A vapor of frog song and creek music rises from the valley floor. The gentle trill of a screech owl falls from the forest behind my right shoulder. Lavender clouds gape above conifer silhouettes. A scant breeze out of the southwest speaks of nothing but rising darkness. Dinner is a warmed-up tamale and last fall's apple. Bourbon for dessert.

Inside the house, tree bones mumble in the woodstove, warming the front room. Beyond the window, clouds swing open to three-quarter Moon, her ivory-skull face averted. She stares off toward some celestial object in the north that I cannot see. Moonlight drifts in like new snow. I exhale, search deeply beneath my sternum. There is only a contented wetness of lungs.

31. Pruning

One year has passed since the beginning of the end of the world we thought we knew. For several days now, the ranks of successive winter rainstorms marching inland off the gray churn of the Pacific have been breached by late March sun. Today on the way up the driveway to the Johnny Gunter place, Kim and I saw the first buttery bloom of wood violets in the moss between the ruts. The front porch thermometer threatens 60 degrees. Squishy pickup tracks in the parking area are beginning to dry and harden, radiating the smell of warming mud. In this newborn spring with a timid sun pushing the margins of darkness away and the storm heave of an entire pandemic year now trailing behind, something inside me has shifted. After two decades of tucking pieces of my soul away into the steadiness of the Coast Range, I've handed my whole heart off to this place.

Since early February I have steadfastly averted my eyes from the exuberant grass jumping the gun on spring and have continued to prune apple trees. Kim has come with me to gather and haul the slender sprouts of once rampant growth to a pile outside the orchard. Beyond her excellent company, she's here for another reason. I need to prune the big King apple tree, aka Man Killer. It is thirty feet tall, ancient trunk peppered with red-breasted sapsucker drills, limbs mossy and drooping with old man's beard lichen. Most of the work can be done with a ladder and a pole pruner, but the topmost branches can be reached only by climbing. I'm not sixty anymore, and if something goes sideways (or rapidly downward), Kim will be here to haul my sorry ass out to the emergency room. Or the morgue.

From my elevated view in the Man Killer, I watch her stooping to pull blackberries from around a large and ancient azalea at the corner of the old house, its pear-colored buds about to burst into spring. From within the density of its unpruned branches a Pacific wren chatters with walnut-size ferocity. I hope that he finds a mate and they will nest there.

When I started pruning at the Johnny Gunter place over a decade ago, the trees were growing feral and unchecked other than by the indiscriminate brutality of bears. My late winter ritual with loppers and a saw has caused me to despise the old pruning metaphors. You know the old axiom, *off with the old wood to encourage new growth*. Anyone who has spent serious time on the arms-end of a pair of loppers knows this is utter bullshit. Most of the old wood stays on the tree. It's the new shoots from the previous growing season that hit the ground in heaps and are carted away to the burn pile.

Maybe my growing disdain for the old-wood/new-wood metaphor is because I'm becoming old wood myself. Besides, the aphorism is ageist. Time for a change. A new outlook on pruning. Old wood provides structure, a framework around which to shape the tree. Old wood guarantees the future of these trees by holding new growth up to the sunlight where it can mature, blossom, and bear fruit. Even ancient wood hollowed out by rot will continue in this supporting capacity. Decay makes trees ever wiser and more diverse. They provide nesting cavities for wrens and chickadees. And when a limb finally breaks off under the weight of wet snow or a hungry bear, the wood makes a final contribution to my smoked salmon.

New wood will make old wood. Over and over. On and on. When Grammy was about ninety, her family took her to southern Arizona for a winter "vacation." When she returned, Mom asked her how her trip was. *Oh, it was nice, but I got tired of being around all those old people!* She meant that she had grown weary of being without any intergenerational diversity. In her last decade, Grammy's brain became confused by memory loss, but she was still able to die at Mom and Dad's. How grateful I am to have been born into a family that nurtures old wood.

The Man Killer has killed no men this year. From the feet-on-the-ground safety of my front yard in town, I snip vertical shoots from a timid dwarf apple tree. Across the street, the neighborhood kids take turns flailing and screaming from swings strung high in a giant pin oak. A couple wanders by with their dog. They moved into the neighborhood at the same time we did, raised a son here. They stop for a few minutes to share their dog with the kids. The woman looks over at me.

Smiles. "It's not so quiet for you these days, is it?"

Nope, it isn't quiet. And I like it. I only hope that when I finally hollow out, the chickadees will move in. Maybe a pair of wrens could nest in the dark gnarl of my chest.

32. PULSE

Infant spring arrives at this place in the mountains where my heart now lies. Low overcast hangs from needled ridges like the teeth of a soft-mouthed dog. Darkness trickles in around the fraying edges of the day. There is no moon, no stars, no lavender sunset. A breeze off the north ridge breathes its last. On the valley floor, chorus frog song mingles with the soft rush of water still retreating from a rainstorm several days ago. On evenings like this, I press my ear tightly against the chest of the mountains and listen for a heartbeat.

My body aches. I spent the day milling siding boards from a Douglas-fir that used to live at the upper edge of the meadow. The tree wasn't large, perhaps 18 inches in diameter, but it rose straight up for 100 feet. Two spots of seeping black rot seemed to signal it was time for the fir to become lumber for putting the aging and decrepit house back together. The mill blade sang through the turpentine pungency of the green log, a plume of fine sawdust spitting to the left. After squaring off the log, I stared at the red heart of the tree wrapped in fifty concentric rings of its former life and struggled a bit with the prospect of reducing the beam to three-quarter-inch boards. But the house needed siding, not beams.

That afternoon, a barred owl laughed from the big trees above the meadow, telltale repeats of *who cooks for you?* The last note bent downward in tone and intensity the way an old vine maple bows beneath its load of winter-soaked moss. I knew the owl was looking for a mate. Yet from somewhere in the wet canyons of my brain, I imagined he was laughing with me, laughing like a good-humored Buddhist at my trifling efforts to hang onto this house for another generation, hang on in the impermanence of a world saturated with rain, a place where the living become so quickly subsumed into the long-suffering cycles of death and decay.

This week my father would have been 92. He would have loved this project, the do-it-yourself logging and making of lumber and makeshift carpentry. He left with a heart I admired and skills I will never have. He would have done a better job falling this tree that for a short time was resting in state on the rails of the mill. My final cut with the chainsaw was flawed. I left too much wood on the uphill side of the hinge and pulled the rapidly falling fir to the right of my chosen path downward. Not a disaster. Just not perfect. But even with his prodigious skills, Dad wasn't able to move forward with rebuilding this house that his own father helped my great-uncle build. His expectations for the project were too high.

The passing of a life necessarily leaves a gaping hole in the forest of the living. When someone leaves us to join the larger cycles of the universe, we grieve the loss of those things we can never know, never become. Yet loss is a requirement of living. Each of us forms a unique bubble of consciousness that persists for only a short time in an otherwise entropic universe, our one-and-only contribution to the world. The living can only reform their lives around the inimitable hole left by our passing.

Soon I'll be leaving these wet and gentle mountains to spend a month in the hard edges and sandstone grit of the Grand Canyon. Big water and adrenaline will carry me down the Colorado River. "They" say I will emerge from the canyon changed. This scares the shit out of me. In this last quarter of my life, I'm just getting comfortable with my place in the world. But an attentive life is a river, always pressing out around the edges, adjusting course, leaving our unique erosional trace in the world. Somewhere along the surge and quietude of the Colorado River, I'll celebrate the third year since Dad's passing. And in that deep incision through the Kaibab Plateau, I'll place my hand on Vishnu Schist 1.8 billion years old, only a bit younger than the beginning of all life. I'll be feeling for the pulse of the earth.

For now, darkness wings in on soft feathers. Two great-horned owls are in soft conversation high on the ridge. A patter of unannounced rain tickles the porch roof. I hold my ear to the chest of these soaking mountains, to the breast of my father, listening for a heartbeat. The monk owl is laughing.

33. Unconformity

Before I left my beloved retreat in the Oregon Coast Range to spend twenty-three days floating by raft and dory through the Grand Canyon, I promised to place my hand on the Vishnu Schist deep within the gorge and check the pulse of the earth. I have done that. The report is complicated. The pulse beneath my fingers was varied: occasionally strong and clear, often faint and barely detectable, sometimes a slow throb or a racing patter or skipped beats or a host of other arrhythmias that I will forever struggle to capture with words.

Vishnu Schist mirrors the complexity of my time in the Canyon. This schist is a mishmash of original materials that include ocean sediments and fiery volcanics born between 1.6 and 1.8 billion years ago. The original rock was folded into the high-pressure heart of the earth and transformed into shiny blackness reminiscent of the obsidian flows in my volcanic homeland. Vishnu is the Hindu deity in charge of the preservation and protection of the Universe. Vishnu was undoubtedly looking out for the Grand Canyon when the ever-busy Bureau of Reclamation was drilling test holes for additional dam sites downstream from Glen Canyon. Those projects were abandoned under intense public outcry.

At Bass Crossing, 109 river miles downstream from our start at Lees Ferry, a licorice wall of schist juts behind our camp kitchen, cut and polished into glistening convolutions by the grit and grind of the River. One concavity is about the dimensions of an upright coffin. When Sun escapes behind towering pink sandstone and our camp sighs into evening shadows, I insert myself into this black sarcophagus and warm my weary bones in the stored heat of the dying day.

In the lower canyon, the Vishnu Complex is overlain by strata hundreds of millions of years younger. The result is massive gaps of missing time in the geological record. Geologists call this the Great Unconformity to distinguish it from a host of smaller unconformities throughout the Canyon. I like the idea of unconformities. They are paradoxes. They make sense only after the underlying process is discerned.

At river mile 148, Matkatamiba Canyon is incised into Mauve Sandstone. Jeweled pools are strewn along the canyon floor and separated by short vertical plunges. A fern finds a toehold in the vertical wall, seemingly kept alive by the smell of dampness. One of my companions is a friend you want to have. He wades to his knees into the deepest pool to leave the ashes of his friend's daughter. She loved the Grand Canyon and was taken too soon by cystic fibrosis. A drift of dry rose petals and ash spread across the transparency of water. Words from the poem "Do Not Stand at My Grave and Weep" float on cool morning air. My friend staggers out of the pool onto a rocky beach, overcome. My own tears well up. Genetics was my career. Yet at times I hate the brutality of it. Even Vishnu offers no protection when things go wrong with our DNA.

That night we camp on the beach at Tuckup Canyon. White noise from 164 Mile Rapid sucks me downward into sleep. I dream that I'm sitting on the edge of my cot. My father is there; not his face, but a felt presence off to my right. The weight of every loss that has ever been settles over my tired shoulders—people now passed, beautiful places destroyed, everything I wouldn't accomplish in the smallness of my life. A turbulence of grief pulls me down. I'm crying beyond any hope of stopping. When I finally struggle to the surface of consciousness, I'm gasping for breath. This is the unconformity that lies at the interface of grief and gratitude. We live and love. We lose. In the end, we become the lost.

River mile 179. Our days have become a numberless procession of feather duster tamarisk, blush of blooming barrel cacti, and the swell and sigh of big water grinding relentlessly downward, undaunted by the rock trying to contain it. I nestle in the front of the raft as we whoosh into Lava Falls, 30 seconds of giant waves and adrenaline once erroneously listed by Guinness as the fastest navigable water in North America. After 15 seconds of exhilaration along a perfect line, the River isn't having it. Our right oar is seized by hydraulics that reduce a human arm to inconsequential flesh, blood, and bone. The oar is slammed upward, jammed with its tether into the oarlock, transformed into the broken stub of a wing. Our raft swings sideways into the first and largest wave of the Big Kahuna near the foot of the rapid. I throw my body against the blue bulge of the high side and vanish beneath the churn of the wave chamber. For a sickening two seconds I'm submerged and vertical in a vessel that should be flat to the river but is now tipped on edge. Vishnu must have been aboard. After clearing the last breaker, the raft is spit upright from the maelstrom with us still inside. Reconnecting with our six compatriots in a downstream eddy, we laugh hysterically, swear hard, and thank the River Spirits by pouring the tops off freshly opened beers into quietly lapping water. Ours is an unconformity of emotions.

The magnitude of space and time in the Grand Canyon imposes itself daily in an ongoing erosion of one's self-importance: schists nearly 2 billion years old; 500 million layered years of sandstone carved by water into rosy buttresses jutting several thousand feet above the river; intrusions of black lava that poured forth in the flick of a geological eyelash 1 million years ago; granaries and dwellings of the

Hisatsinom, ancestral Puebloans, tunneled into the rock a mere thousand years ago. On this scale of reality, my twenty-three days of gawk and awe become only a glimmer of bioelectricity traveling along an overstimulated nerve cell.

Somewhere in this immensity of rock, water, and sky lies a spiritual unconformity waiting for a human to happen upon it. Yes, a single life can vanish in the vastness. But the tiny heartbeat that maintains our ephemeral purchase on this planet becomes even more miraculous, more powerful, more important. Conscious attentiveness washes away nihilism, sending it downstream to be dropped on a sandy beach where it awaits transformation into something new. Only our voice remains—glistening, radiant, sometimes dark. Our hard edges are polished smooth by the relentless gentling hands of those who reach out to us. We become ourselves.

***

Back home, I'm swallowed in the damp dusk of an unseasonably cool Coast Range evening. I collapse into the plastic lawn chair on the front porch, hunch into my ancient down parka, and reach out to the unconformities of nightfall in newly hatched May. Rattle of ice cubes, hot flush of bourbon. Spring bird chorus muted by earlier rain. Swainson's thrush sending his upwardly bending *weep* into the gloom but without his full-throated spiraling voice. Salmon-flank clouds airbrushed onto the cobalt horizon swim slowly south on a north wind. Moon half-full, pocked with silence, inscrutable between cloud layers. The lawnmowers are broken down. Contentment sifts into every pore.

34. Dawn Chorus

Awake at 4 a.m. Chilly air eddies through my open bedroom window at the Johnny Gunter house, swirling the residue of an uncomfortable dream already forgotten. My nocturnal amnesia is a blessing—those unconscious wanderings are mostly baggage shed by an overburdened brain. To remember them would be like clutching a suitcase filled with extraneous junk. No dreamcatcher for me, thank you. Just an open window to the forest through which those fugitives from my subconscious can escape. There they can take on a new identity, be absorbed and transformed like carbon dioxide taken up by fresh summer needle growth.

At 4:30 I give up on sleep. Night-scrubbed stars fade in the glow of the infant day. A few bird calls drift through the window, bubbles of sound riding the growing current of light. With coffee and an energy bar in hand, I find my way to the front porch. Though summer is nearly here, 45 degrees makes a mockery of my canvas jacket, and I retrieve the old down parka hanging inside the house. The dawn chorus rises in earnest, a density of voices that defies my need to dissect and identify individual birdsongs. This morning the birds seem farther from the porch, as though the they have distanced themselves. Sip of coffee. Small breath. Ears surrender to the wholeness of high-pitched tweets, mid-range chitters, and hoarse buzzes. From an unseen ridge to the north, a high-lead logging whistle pierces the birdsong. I wonder for a moment how many active nests were destroyed by that clearcut. This is why my dreams are sometimes disturbing.

Even though unknown future rolls out into space-time, from this tenuous anchor in the *now* I can wrap my head around the near-term details. They aren't earth shattering. I'll finish scribbling in my journal, drain my coffee, scrape the last oatmeal with blueberries out of the bowl, then fire up the DR brush mower. A quarter-acre concavity just west of the garden fence hasn't been mowed this spring, and the grass there is tall enough to hide a leopard. In the past, that low place with precipitous sides beat the hell out of my riding lawnmower. Now I'm forced to beat the hell out of myself by clinging to the handles of the DR mower. Those steeps sides were created back in 1949 when my ancestors built the house. When the home site and parking area were leveled, they pushed the leftover dirt into the head of the hollow. Before white people came, this spot was probably a depression in a shady old forest where cold water seeped quietly around drooping clumps of maidenhair fern on its trickling path toward the valley floor. My mind dodges into the past. I wonder how many bird nests were destroyed when the land was first cleared all those decades ago. One cost of attentiveness is the realization that none of us can negotiate all of the ridges and canyons of our lives and remain unsullied by human-caused harm, even damage incurred generations ago. We can only forgive, strive for change, and move forward.

My aging body is becoming increasingly enamored of power tools. Managing the Johnny Gunter place with what remains of my life has become untenable without the roar of engines that burn my grandchildren's fossil fuel inheritance. And yet the prospect of starting the DR causes a tinge of remorse. The

Briggs and Stratton engine will drown out the birdsong and set the barn swallows who nest in the garage into flight. Last night, the 19-horsepower Kohler engine that drives the portable sawmill seemed to sense my ambivalence and tried to help by inexplicably dying while I sawed 2 × 4s for the house project. My rational side thought there was moisture in the fuel. Another part of me believed the engine was giving the barn swallows a break from the noise. Later, I discovered that my grandson, with the inexplicable reasoning of a three-year-old, had chosen to close the valve in the fuel hose.

Morning spools out. I scrunch further into the old parka, trying to stay present while trying to stay warm. Sun breaches an unnamed ridge behind the house. Tangerine light coats the clearcuts and conifer silhouettes on the southwest ridges. New sunlight unwraps the dawn sky like a summer-blue iris. On the north ridge, the old Douglas-firs change from orange to lemon. The bird chorus wanes. I begin to recognize old friends: squawk of Steller's Jay, throaty bark of Raven, burble of Black-headed Grosbeak, and the vaporous voice of Swainson's Thrush swirling into the brightening sky.

The chill cools my coffee, stiffens my fingers. On this pandemic morning that chases the heels of my troubled dreams, with birdsong broken by a logging whistle and the remaining tranquility about to be shattered under the auditory hammer of a gasoline engine, I am stupefied by my good fortune. Whether by accident or intention or destiny or all of the above, I have chosen this messy life where everything matters. What a privilege. I slip inside the house, crawl into bed, and sleep for two more hours.

www.ingramcontent.com/pod-product-compliance
Lightning Source LLC
Chambersburg PA
CBHW060400080526
44583CB00012B/398